Grace Halphen is fifteen years old and halfway through Year 10 at Wesley College in Melbourne. She began *Letter to My Teenage Self* while at another high school after she'd had a difficult time transitioning there from primary school. That experience made her want to create something to help people who are going through similar challenges.

Letter to my TEENAGE SELF

EDITED BY GRACE HALPHEN

OUTSTANDING AUSTRALIANS SHARE THE ADVICE
THEY WISH THEY'D BEEN GIVEN GROWING UP

Affirmpress
books that leave an impression

Published by Affirm Press in 2016
28 Thistlethwaite Street, South Melbourne, VIC 3205.
www.affirmpress.com.au

10 9 8 7 6

A catalogue record for this
book is available from the
National Library of Australia

Title: Letter to My Teenage Self / Grace Halphen, editor.
ISBN: 9781925475067 (paperback)

Cover design by Karen Wallis
Typeset in Garamond Premier Pro 12/18.5 by J&M Typesetting
Proudly printed in Australia by Griffin Press

The paper this book is printed on is certified against the Forest Stewardship
Council® Standards. Griffin Press holds FSC chain of custody certification
SGS-COC-005088. FSC promotes environmentally responsible, socially
beneficial and economically viable management of the world's forests.

Contents

Introduction

Being young is hard. Everything is unknown, everyone else's opinions seem to matter and little speed bumps cause collateral damage.

When I first moved to secondary school, this was exactly the case for me. Girls were mean, social media dictated my every move and I desperately wanted to fit in, but I never felt that I did. This all seemed like the end of the world, and I just couldn't see that I wasn't the only one feeling like I was on the outside. I wish I knew then that most of my classmates were just as uncomfortable as I was. It felt impossible to leave the house each morning for school, and I couldn't even say why. Nothing was really wrong, but nothing ever felt right either. I was very unhappy, and that's not a good way to be feeling for a long time.

I think that when you're at your worst, advice can go straight over your head. You just want to know that everything is going to be okay. The problem is, though, that people can tell you this all they want, but you know there's no way that they could know it for sure.

I felt frustrated and angry a lot. I didn't know why school wasn't working out for me, so I couldn't take anything on board to try and make it all better. Letting other people see how I was really feeling was my worst nightmare. I thought that if I put up with the discomfort for a little bit longer, everything would brighten up. But that was like leaving a wound open for more bacteria and dirt to get inside; it just made things worse.

I don't think it's okay for anyone to be stuck in a sad place for a long time like I was. I felt like no one could possibly understand what I was going through, because to be honest, I didn't fully understand it either.

It was even more frustrating to know that everyone around me seemed assured that I was going to somehow feel better, but I couldn't see it that way at all. It seemed that I would be stuck in that place forever.

Getting ready to face my final years of schooling, I'd be lying if I said that things were perfect. But after learning how to deal with the discomfort, things are getting better. A few years ago, it would have been so reassuring to have known for sure that it was all going to turn out fine.

In creating this book, I don't expect to provide instant relief to young people out there going through the same things that I did. I know from experience that it only feels overwhelming when advice is coming from every direction, despite everyone's good intentions. When you're feeling as bad as I was, the only person who can convince you that things will get better is yourself.

While I know that I can't make people feel instantly okay, I'd like this book to provide support to anyone feeling low. Other people out there who have struggled at some point in their lives have gone on to do amazing things, which is possible for anyone, regardless of what they may be going through. Being young can be hard, but it's a journey that we've all got in common.

Martin Halphen is Grace's dad.

Dear Marty,

You've probably often heard that youth is wasted on the young. You'd be happy to hear that I believe that is so untrue. Unfortunately it's more a case of experience wasted by the old.

Admittedly we're not familiar with too much when we're young, but navigating through the unknown and often outside your comfort zone is truly one of life's greatest journeys.

Being prepared to make mistakes, trial and error, blind courage and fearlessness are too many times lost when we've seen too much.

However, our innocence when we're young is just a beautiful humility that keeps our mind open to the countless opportunities that come our way.

It's a time when our senses are alive and, yes, sometimes our feelings are overwhelmingly uncertain and vulnerable. But working through these struggles is what will eventually define you and make all the successes you have worthwhile.

Work towards knowing who you are, which is just incredibly powerful. It really isn't so difficult. Just be guided by what makes you feel good and anything that gives you energy. Such insight will help you identify what you need to nurture, and the outcome will gift you a heart that loves – yourself first, which will be followed by love for others and the world around you.

So take care of yourself, young fella. Keep that mind restless, continue making mistakes but never make the same mistake twice. Any motivation shouldn't be about perfection, as this simply doesn't exist. But being the best you can be is always within reach. Celebrate the wins hard, learn from the losses and, above everything else, always be kind and love unconditionally.

ADAM
GILCHRIST

Adam ('Gilly') Gilchrist was one of the most exciting cricketers of his generation and is widely regarded as the greatest wicket-keeper–batsman in the history of the game. He grew up in Lismore, New South Wales, and now lives in Perth. He played in ninety-six Tests for Australia between 1999 and 2008, and is a former chair of the National Australia Day Council.

Dear Adam,

Welcome to the teenage years. The good stuff is about to begin. But before you read any further, go and have a music lesson. Don't care what instrument, but please learn to play something, and keep at it, well into adulthood. Good.

I can understand you may feel the next few years of your life are pretty daunting. Many of a similar age also see it that way. It doesn't have to be, I promise.

It's all in your attitude. You see, attitudes are contagious and every day you should ask yourself the question, 'Is your attitude worth catching?' From the moment you wake up, to whatever it is you are doing throughout each day, it's your attitude that will either make it a good experience or a crap one. How you think is how you'll feel is how you'll act. Say this over a few times, slowly in your mind. It makes sense and it will help you learn a great deal, even when you least expect it.

On a different note, what about all the different-looking kids around at the moment? All the changing body shapes, some tall, some still short. Fatter, thinner, darker, lighter. And some of the clothing choices kids are making! Through choice or custom, whatever the case, they don't look normal, do they?

Well, mate, let me give you a tip: there is no such thing as normal. There is no set mould. There are 7 billion of us and we are all different. That's what makes it all so interesting.

There will be kids you cross paths with who have differing interests to yours. Different tastes or points of view. Don't bag them out. Don't tease them or make fun of them in front of others or, even worse, behind their back. Just remember, whatever you are doing to others, someone else could be doing to you, so either make it positive or leave them alone to enjoy their time. It's called respect. Always be respectful. It can be easy to forget this, but try hard.

Remember a few years back, when playing your dad in a game of chess you 'stole' his queen off the board whilst he was out of the room getting a drink. Pretty silly idea, eh, as he noticed straight away and asked if you pinched it, and foolishly you said, 'No, no, I legally took it in the match earlier.' Wasn't worth it, was it? Dad hated making you pack away your sporting gear and banning you from sport until you confessed the truth, but he had to teach you that it's not cool to steal or cheat. I guess it was only a game of chess, but mate, we make a lot of decisions every day, and we all hope to make more good decisions than bad ones. A good way to achieve this is always think what effect on others your actions will have. Before you say something, think about whether it will offend someone else. Respect.

Finally, don't carry around a backpack that is overloaded and too heavy for you. It will cause long-term damage to your spine that may take quite a while to get better. In fact, whilst on that subject, don't carry an overloaded mind around too long either. If there is something bugging you, talk about it. Something you don't understand? Ask. A fear? Discuss it and formulate a plan. Always communicate. This is so important in every aspect of your life ahead. Talk, type, write, sing, whatever. Just please communicate. Because like your back and neck from the heavy backpack, the mind and heart can be seriously damaged if overloaded for too long and can take a long time to heal. Communicate. Often the issue you see as a big deal is no issue at all, but until you talk to someone about it, you'll never know.

So have fun, buddy, because if it ain't fun, it ain't worth doing. Even the long, boring subjects at school can be fun if taken on with the right attitude. Read lots, exercise just as much. Laugh at yourself, it's good for the soul.

You've got it all ahead of you, such an exciting journey, a successful journey, if approached with the right attitude, with respect and if you consistently communicate with those around you.

Oh, did I mention learning music? Let's face it ... Rockstars are cool!!

With love,

Adam

ALEX
MILES

Alex (Lee) Miles is a Melbourne-based author who has worked across theatre, television and advertising, including as a scriptwriter and storyliner for *Neighbours*. She has published eight books in the *Zac Power* series. Her book *Sixty Secrets for a Happy Bride* was published by Affirm Press in 2015, and she is working on *Starring Olive Black*, a children's fiction series to be published by Affirm in 2017.

Dearest ALpal,

I'm writing you this letter twenty years in the future, while sunbaking on the moon in my tinfoil bikini – everyone's doing it. Writing letters and lists has become a bit of a pastime for us. Keep it up! They'll help you feel grateful for all you have, drive you to reach your goals and provide a hearty giggle when you read them back years later.

Things are bad, I know, with Mum's illness just being diagnosed. You'll swing between feeling lost, sad, thankful, angry, alone, hopeful, defeated and wondering, 'Why me?' All of these feelings are valid. And it's mighty important that you share them. It might be with Kelly, or the girls, or Ms Illesca at school, or Dad. Or write yourself a letter. Heck, talk to Teddy too. He may only have one ear but he'll listen. There is always someone who will listen.

You can't undo what's happened to Mum, but the most marvellous consolation prize is working out from a young age the importance of grabbing life with both hands. You never know what's around the corner, so do things that make your knees wobble or your heart pound. Laugh – always laugh. And make sure the people you love are reminded of it every day, with both words and actions. Yes, you read these sentiments on fortune cookies and T-shirts from Bali – but they're so true.

When it comes to friendships, you can't get everything you need in life from just one person. It's okay, healthy even, to have different types of friends. There'll be ones that challenge you. Ones that understand your chocolate obsession. Ones to dance with. Ones to be still with. Ones from school and ones that aren't. Ones that you see all the time.

Others rarely, but it's like no time has passed. True friends adore the *real* you no matter what. Work out who these ones are, and which friends give you the best advice, even the stuff you'd rather not hear. The others might not be keepers, but they'll colour your life as they move in and out of it.

Spoiler alert – you're a worrier. You worry so much that you need lists to keep track of them. Just remember there's a finite amount of space in your life for worry, so be selective. Leave out the ones that are not in your control, or really far in the future. Writing them down will help manage it some days. Having a good sleep helps too. And try asking yourself, '*Why* am I worried?' Is it because you're scared of letting someone down? Or because you've set yourself a challenge? When you can't work out why, it's a good time to chat to someone. Worrying is both your best and worst trait – you can't switch it off completely, but you can learn which ones are worth the energy.

For someone who's a terrible reader and terrible speller with terrible handwriting, you'll laugh when you learn what career path you take. Don't overthink it at school. Say yes to every opportunity and do what you love. You never know where it'll lead you. Speaking of which, I loved reading back over your Year 7 Time Capsule. You were spot on with some predictions and rubbish at others, but there's no way I'm telling you which were which. Working it out and all the mistakes along the way are what make life so super.

I'll leave you with some bad news I heard recently: 'time flies'. The good news, though, is that you're the pilot. Travel safe and have fun!

Lots of love,

Alex

ALICE
PUNG

Alice Pung is a writer and lawyer who grew up in Footscray, Melbourne. She won Newcomer of the Year in the 2007 Australian Book Industry Awards for her first memoir, *Unpolished Gem*. Her second memoir, *Her Father's Daughter*, won the WA Premier's Book Award for Non-fiction. *Laurinda*, her first novel, won the Ethel Turner Prize for Young People's Literature at the 2016 NSW Premier's Literary Awards.

Dear Alice,

You've changed schools this year, and even though you have assiduously studied *TV Hits* and *Smash Hits* magazines over the summer so that you might fit in, you will soon realise that knowing things is not the same as being able to talk about them to other girls. You are scared and timid, but these two upcoming years at Christ the King College will be the best years of your high school education out of the five different high schools you attend. You will go on resilience camps, and join the choir, and meet two of your best friends, Lisa and Elizabeth, whose weddings you will attend in a little over a decade's time. You will come to understand that a school can really shape a person in terms of its values, even though it is located in one of the poorest neighbourhoods in Victoria.

You will meet girls who are strong and funny and loud. You will spend many afternoons in the homes of your friends whose parents – like your own – work in garages, as mechanics and outworkers. You will see your friends do adult tasks like call up electricity companies for their parents who can't speak English, or enrol younger siblings in high school. You will be part of a community at Christ the King College where your background and circumstances don't matter so much as your kindness and concern for others. And then when you leave this school in two years' time, you will miss it for the rest of your high school days.

Your future self has a sweet husband named Nick and a baby, eight months old, named Leo. You married Nick not because of outer-worldly success, but for his inner qualities of kindness and calm and patience.

You also write books for children and young adults, because during your most formative and lonely years, when you felt most powerless and yet most reflective about the world, young adult authors helped you weather the storm. They showed you the possibilities of thinking beyond your own small world, and taught you not to be judgmental of others through their stories of different characters' interior worlds. You will also visit hundreds of high schools and speak to thousands of students, and some of them will feel less lonely for it.

I will not lie. The future will not be a breeze. You will encounter failure along the way, and a great tragedy. You will, however, maintain a sense of hope through the loss. As an adult, you will feel more empowered to deal with what life brings into your path, and a sense of resilience. Life will teach you to appreciate the small joys, and how to extend compassion because you have experienced suffering. You will keep on keeping on, and try to be a better Buddhist. And you will keep writing through it all.

BERRY LIBERMAN

Berry Liberman, who grew up in Melbourne, is the editor and publisher of *Dumbo Feather* magazine and co-founder of Small Giants, which nurtures and empowers businesses that are focused on a more socially equitable and environmentally sustainable world.

Dear teenage Berry,

Everything is going to be alright. I promise. You will have a long and sometimes challenging journey – a bit like *Lord of the Rings*, with some bad monsters, some kind friends, a few wise teachers and a guardian wizard or two. It will totally be worth it.

I know you like instant gratification! You want what you want NOW. I'm afraid you will have to learn to love the journey, not the end point. This will be very hard for you because you want things to be perfect – but bad luck, kiddo! Nothing is perfect, no one is perfect and it is better to do something than not do it because you're afraid it won't be good enough. DO IT ANYWAY. If you're worried what your mum will think, or your dad, or your sister or brother or friends or the cute boy in English class ... well, that's a waste of time. The truth is that the people who end up having a good time and a good life are the ones who show up. The ones who care – who have passion and put their whole hearts into things. It may not be cool right now – but what's cool in year seven and eight isn't cool when you're older.

Things right now for you are okay, but soon something really bad is going to happen ... I can't tell you what but it will change your world. It will be very sad. When things are sad you have to take care of yourself. Do nice things. Read good books, watch great movies, write, be inspired, spend time with the people you love, get lots of sleep and eat nourishing food. DON'T BE HARD ON YOURSELF. Lie down on the grass in the sunshine and let the earth hold you up if you're having a hard day. Don't give any time to mean and nasty people. Just keep walking. You can't be liked by everyone so don't even try. I promise you everything is going to be alright. You need to trust in yourself. Make friends with people who love you for who you are, not what you have or what you can do for them.

Don't be afraid to immerse yourself in your books and your music and lots and lots of daydreaming. It's important because once you become a grown-up there's so much pressure to stop daydreaming. About boys – well, the good news is you will go out with a few who aren't so right for you but in the end you will find the best boy in the world. He will think of you as his equal. He will want to share with you everything. Your happiness and your sadness, your strengths and your weaknesses. He will be kind, and that is the most important thing. He will support your work, your creative life, having a family – all of it. It will be fun and life can be full of love once you learn to trust yourself. Before you meet him, though – HAVE LOTS OF FUN!

You will go on big journeys into the world and into your soul. It is important. Don't panic. Growing up is going to require a lot of thoughtful navigation. School is only a short time in a long life – make it count. Sign up for choir and the play and be brave and laugh a lot.

This may not make sense right now but remember this: Comparison is the death of happiness – so just be yourself. Sending you mountains of love from twenty-five years in the future,

Berry xox

CHET
FAKER

Nick Murphy, better known as Chet Faker, is an electronica musician hailing from Melbourne, who's now based in Brooklyn. He won five 2014 ARIA Awards including Best Male Artist, Producer of the Year and Best Independent Release. He also took the Number 1 spot in the 2014 triple j Hottest 100.

Hi Dude,

I don't want to give too much away, because the journey is more fun than the knowledge.

But one thing that might help you relax is the fact that nobody knows what they are doing. That I can guarantee.

There are people who say they do, and they don't. There are also people who say they don't, and they occasionally do.

Nobody of worth has ever started anything they knew how to do fully.

You're going to figure this out anyway, but you'll read a book by Robert Pirsig that will have a big influence on your life.

That lesson is simple. You can figure out life, or you can live it. Ironically, the latter will help you do the former but that's irrelevant for now.

I have no regrets, which means I don't really want to give you much specific guidance.

Just know that your ego is not the key to happiness, and it's okay to simply let things be; not because they are right or wrong but because they are.

Life is what it is, and meaning is defined after that, so you're better off going with the flow.

You are not your thoughts. You are not your emotions. Lean Into It.

CHRIS JUDD

Chris Judd is a former professional Australian rules footballer, and captain of both the Carlton Football Club and the West Coast Eagles in the AFL. Judd has twice won the league's highest individual honour, the Brownlow Medal, and is a dual Leigh Matthews Trophy winner as the AFL Players Association's Most Valuable Player.

Dear Chris,

Your teenage years are an exciting time to be alive, as is every other year of your life as none of us are around for all that long. Try to both recognise and enjoy the good moments in your life when they arise.

I write this letter to you as your senior by 19 years, but unfortunately at the ripe old age of 32, there is still much to learn, and still plenty of answers I'm waiting to find. Whilst not holding all the answers, there are a few things I've picked up since I was sitting in your shoes that may be helpful in your journey from boy to man.

The first is that kids are terrified of being different from everyone else, while adults are terrified of being the same. While it is tragic to see a kid pretend to be someone they're not purely to fit in, the same can be said for people who pretend to be something they're not purely to be different. Being different or common are neither good nor bad character traits: being authentic is what matters. Doing things that you're passionate about while spending time with people who you like, find interesting and trust, and who treat you how you want to be treated is the best way to go.

Secondly, what gets respected by your peers is transient and constantly changing. Don't chase it. When I was your age, the guys who were most respected (as measured by the amount of interest they received from girls) were guys who wagged or dropped out of school, got into trouble, etc. But by the time everyone was 18 they were less impressed with these guys, and the crowd was after a different hero. Depending on what age you are there is always a new hero to be revered. In your thirties and forties it may be the entrepreneur with the biggest bank balance who's most respected by others his age, but while being an entrepreneur can be a noble pursuit, if it has come at the cost of his family, then maybe the pursuit wasn't worth the cost. From what I can gather, there are very few things you can confidently do to excess without paying a heavy price for it later on. The few things that spring to mind are spending time with your family, being healthy (not to be confused with being vain) and learning. Every other pursuit should be weighed up as to what the cost is against these three things.

And lastly, enjoy your hair, you'll start losing it in six years!

All the best,

Chris

DANNII
MINOGUE

Dannii Minogue, who grew up in the Melbourne suburb of Surrey Hills, is a singer–songwriter, talent competition judge, actress, and TV and radio personality. Dannii is most widely known for her roles in the Australian television talent show *Young Talent Time* and *Home and Away*, and her work as a musician and judge on Australia's *The X Factor*.

Dear teenage Dannii,

You've been a career girl for years now so you don't need me to explain to you the value of hard work or tell you that spending 95 per cent of your time tweaking this, learning that, or paying attention to the teeny-tiny details makes that 5 per cent of the time you get to do the thing you love most immeasurably exciting and rewarding.

You've already experienced things other teenagers with stars in their eyes can only dream of, but I want you to know that just as there are even more amazing times ahead of you, there will be some tough times as well. Know that they're a natural part of life, and that when you go through difficult times, you have to go through all of the emotions.

You're like a rainbow and every colour and shade is beautiful from dark and stormy to light and sparkling. It's okay to be those different colours of emotions – each of them is a part of you and they're what make you beautiful. Trying to suppress or hide them doesn't improve you, how you're feeling, or how people see you. Let all your colours shine though.

It's okay to sometimes feel upset or alone. Just try not to get stuck in the dark place. Don't stay there.

Feel it, live it, move on.

Don't fear failure or try to avoid it by giving up the things you're passionate about if they're not easy. The people you like, admire and look up to the most have all tried, failed, and got up and tried again on their journey to be the best at what they do.

So, when an unfeasibly successful entertainment guru tells you, 'It's as much from your failures as any of your successes that you've made it where you are today,' heed his wisdom, have faith in yourself and take the plunge. In fact, jump in feet first whenever you're presented with a new opportunity whether you know what you're doing or not (and you generally won't).

Your life will be richer for it.

Don't be afraid to make mistakes, look silly, or show your vulnerability. People relate to your mistakes, and your vulnerability is what helps them feel a connection with you. And make sure you're receptive when others show their vulnerability. Only good can come of that.

Try to remember that perfection doesn't exist. It's an ideal, not a reality, although I can promise you that you're going to get a lot of fun and fulfilment out of striving for it.

Lastly, did you know that people asked to list the top 10 things they love rarely put themselves on that list? Make sure you're on your list!

Dannii x

DAVID
KOCH

David 'Kochie' Koch presents as a co-host on
Seven Network's *Sunrise* breakfast program on
weekdays. He has published several bestselling
books, including *Kochie's Guide to Keeping it
Real,* and has been a highly regarded finance
journalist for more than twenty years.

Dear David,

Have enough confidence in yourself to give anything a go ... but if it doesn't work out, have enough confidence in yourself to go and do something else.

What a life you're going to have. It will be the most exciting, invigorating and tumultuous period in history. Technology will change your world forever and the pace at which it's going to change will blow your mind.

It's going to be great. It's going to be exciting. But it's up to you to embrace it, to love the challenge ... and have enough confidence in yourself to make it work for you.

Do not fear change. See it as an amazing opportunity to make a difference and to improve yourself as a person. Learn to love change.

The world is going to get a whole lot smaller, you'll be bombarded with information ... so much information. So be inquisitive and have a passion for learning throughout your life.

But with all this change, with all this new technology, with all this excitement, with all this distraction, your biggest challenge is going to be staying true to yourself.

Your life will be defined by who you want to be as a person and whether you have the guts to be true to yourself. It won't be easy.

While technology, change and innovation can make the world smaller it can also make us more self-absorbed and antisocial, and stifle individualism.

Start forming and thinking about your values now. Because it's those values which will define not only your life but also how you measure success, failure and achievement.

Look around you for role models, who you admire, to help define your values. Be wary of people whose fame or money defines their success or values. Look below the surface. What do they do for others? Are they kind? Do they respect others (no matter who they are)? Are they proud of their own values and stick to them?

I've learnt that the more someone does for others, the better the person they are. And it's usually the little things ... helping an elderly neighbour put their garbage bins out, volunteering for a community group, being respectful to others, supporting someone being pressured by their peer group to change good values.

Often it's hard to find those types of mentors because what they do for others isn't always obvious. They don't boast about helping someone else, they just do it. And that's what makes them a good person.

But when you do see someone with these qualities, who cares for others, talk to them, observe them and work out what's good for you.

You're going to have to fight to be a good person. There will be plenty of distractions and people who want you to be like them. But you're not ... you're you.

You have the opportunity to achieve so much. But it's up to you, no one else. Be you. Be proud of you. And never let anyone pressure you into not being ... you.

ELISE
BIALYLEW

Elise Bialylew is a coach, mindfulness meditation teacher and social entrepreneur who trained as a doctor and psychiatrist. After studying with some of the leading meditation teachers in the world, she started a global meditation movement and founded Mindful in May, a global mindfulness movement that has taught thousands of people to meditate, while raising money to build clean water wells in the developing world. She is the author of *The Mindful Month* and teaches mindfulness to corporates at The Mind Life Project.

Dear teenage me,

There are so many things I've learned over the past four decades and although I know you're probably going to have to make some of the same mistakes that I made in order to discover the lessons and wisdom, I hope these words may land in your heart and somehow make the path to your greatest happiness a little more direct.

I know how school can be so challenging at times – not only the work but also the social side of things. I want you to know that 'fitting in' is overrated. Being open to people you don't immediately feel drawn to at school and taking risks to have new conversations (even if you're scared of being rejected) is one of the biggest gifts you can give yourself. You might be surprised about the new and unexpected friendships you make – and of course just remember everyone is just as insecure as you feel – they'll be grateful that you had the courage to take the risk and make the first move towards them. Many of the 'cool people' on the school oval often end up being the least interesting later on.

As for your life path and career, I know it's a terrible cliché and you've probably heard it before but please follow your deepest passions and curiosities – even if they don't seem like viable career paths. A person fuelled by passion can literally change the world (without a degree or PhD) and make the unimaginable happen. Pursuing security is overrated and often leads to a sick soul. Trust me, I've tried both paths and I want to save you the burden. Trust and passion make for a much more solid, fulfilling life than being driven by fear.

There will be many people who try and support you in making the 'right' or 'best' decisions. Your parents will likely be a dominant force in your life. However, as well-meaning as they mean to be, realise they don't know the 'right' answer for you. Know that there are truly no 'right' answers or decisions – and most decisions you make in life are reversible anyway. Learn to trust your own likes, dislikes and callings early in life – they are your most reliable guide.

Reach out sooner rather than later to people who aren't your family for advice and perspectives – maybe a counsellor or life coach or someone in the world you admire. Don't be afraid to write to someone you don't know – people are more than happy to share their wisdom.

Make mistakes and take risks in the face of uncertainty – it's better to spend time getting back on track after discovering you've taken a wrong turn, than end up regretting decisions not made and risks not taken.

Don't plan too far ahead as the world is changing way too quickly for long-term plans. But seriously consider empowering yourself for the future by learning the most powerful language on the planet – computer code.

Know that in order to experience your greatest happiness you'll need to spend as much time doing the inner work of learning how to manage your mind and emotions, as the outer work required to pass your school and university exams.

Learn an inner skill like meditation which will help you to be less fearful and more courageous in the face of the inevitable stresses and challenges that will come your way. Just like you brush your teeth each day, practise gratitude and purposely notice what is good in your life as a way of maintaining your mental hygiene – it's a simple but powerful practice to greater happiness.

Learn how to be your own best friend, rather than be your biggest critic – it could be the most important ingredient for your own wellbeing.

Finally, you will face so many questions and uncertainties as you move forward into your life. Know that the answers will arrive in time and, as frustrating as not knowing what to do is, remind yourself that patience is sometimes all that is required in order to get to the next place you are supposed to be. We've all been in that place of confusion, not knowing and frustration – you are not alone.

As Rainer Maria Rilke famously shared:

> Be patient toward all that is unsolved in your heart and try to love the questions themselves, like locked rooms and like books that are now written in a very foreign tongue. Do not now seek the answers, which cannot be given you because you would not be able to live them. And the point is, to live everything. Live the questions now. Perhaps you will then gradually, without noticing it, live along some distant day into the answer.

ELLIOT
COSTELLO

Elliot Costello is a social entrepreneur who co-founded the YGAP in 2008. YGAP finds and supports impact entrepreneurs with bold solutions to poverty in the world's toughest communities. Elliot grew up in St Kilda, Melbourne, and is the son of Tim Costello, the CEO of World Vision and one of Australia's most recognised voices on social justice, leadership and ethics.

Dear Elliot,

Being 13 is a challenging time of your life. I write to you with the same numbers in my age, but reversed.

I see the frustration you hold. You are leaving St Kilda Primary, so far the home of your education, and you are heading to secondary school. Unlike your friends at St Kilda Primary, you are not going to the local high school or Catholic boys' college. Mum and Dad have, to your dismay, selected Caulfield Grammar School for you.

You are the *only* one from your entire school heading to Caulfield Grammar. The shock and anxiety is real. Every morning you will be boarding from platform two at Balaclava train station while your friends prance around platform one. Make peace with it, though. This is the best decision your parents will make for you.

There is a saying: 'The only constant in life is change.' You won't know it now, but take my word that it's true; and the sooner you comprehend it, the better.

Year Seven will be full of surprises. You find friends quickly, but take stock of who you associate with. It won't be long before some of your 'friends' are requested to leave CGS. Teachers are fond of you but their patience with you will grow thin at times. The small piece of comfort you hold in that first year is choosing your sporting focus: basketball, football and cross-country running. Sport will continue to play a huge role in your life, so be grateful for your opportunities.

I know you're feeling embarrassed. From time to time, you may even feel oppositional. Why do you have the boring father: a Baptist minister? He's a Christian do-gooder who calls the most marginalised people in the community 'friends of the family'. And he even makes the news for doing so from time to time. While all of your friends' parents are pursuing legal, business and medical careers, you sheepishly whisper your father's occupation. This faith that your father holds will begin to resonate with you personally some years from now. Eventually, you will profess to holding it for yourself.

The embarrassment is heightened when your new group of friends stay over at your place for the first time. Peter, a member of the community with mental illness, knocks at the door of your home. You know him, as Mum and Dad often offer him a cup of tea or quiet chat. You explain to him that Mum and Dad are away. While this is normal for you, your friends are shocked. It's the first time you realise how different your upbringing is to that of your new friends from Brighton, Hampton and Sandringham.

It will surprise you to know that the love both your parents provide to our society's most vulnerable, poor and disadvantaged will be a source of inspiration not only to you, but also many of your friends. For some, it will help shape and mould the careers they elect to pursue.

I encourage you now to embrace the difference. Own it. Be proud of your parents and the courageous – albeit different – lives they have chosen to lead.

Before long, you'll be faced with some major peer pressures: kissing girls, drinking alcohol, wagging school and even breaking the law. Some of these experiences are not ideal; but all of them will help shape you.

There is one thing I will warn you against, though: smoking marijuana. It's hard for you to understand right now – it's accepted, or even *encouraged*, among your friends. But this innocent green plant poses the single biggest threat to you and all that you hold dear.

As a person who loves life – his family, friends and sport – you will be harmed by marijuana more than you think. It will burn small holes in your brain. Your studies will suffer. Your friendships will alter. You will become paranoid. Voices will appear. The way you engage with girls at a formative age will change. And it won't be until you form an addiction, which takes two years to shake, that you realise how affected you are by this 'experiment'.

I urge you to say 'no'. Like some other friends, have the courage to resist this path. You are already different from everyone else; this is merely another way to embrace it.

Growing up in St Kilda – a multicultural, lower socioeconomic suburb of Melbourne – you will see many things others won't. You will waste hours hanging out with friends at an arcade parlour run by drug dealers. You will be exposed to street violence and vandalism. You will disrespect authority. All of which seem normal to you. All of which keep your mother awake at night. And rightly so! You will one day lose a close friend in a stolen car, which crashed after a high-speed chase with the police.

The journey ahead is paved for you, Elliot. While turbulence lies ahead over the next few years – both within school and out – you are loved by so many around you. Teachers grant you asylum. You begin to settle down by Year 10 and grow into a sporting leader, high academic achiever and a well-loved member of Caulfield Grammar, all the while binding your old primary school friends into your new social network.

Take heart in your restlessness. Be kinder to yourself. Become a

leader earlier in your life by saying 'no'. And learn to embrace change –
or even welcome it.

Every decision you make enables 'us' to become the man I am today.

Enjoy your teenage years,

Elliot

ERIK
THOMSON

Erik Thomson is a Scottish-born, New Zealand-raised Australian actor. He is known for his roles in the TV series *Hercules: The Legendary Journeys*, *All Saints* and *Packed to the Rafters*. He won an Australian Film Institute Award for his performance in the feature film *Somersault*.

Dear Erik,

Could you please stop watching one-day cricket for a minute and read this letter, it's very important. Okay, now a lot of the things I tell you won't really sink in because you are a teenager and therefore developmentally predisposed to ignore adults' advice. The world is your oyster at your age. You feel immortal and you think you know best how to live your life. I understand that, I've been thirteen myself, just try and absorb that for a start.

There are a few things, however, that would be very helpful for you to at least consider. They may save you some pain, although that said, pain is an elemental part of learning and unavoidable if you're living your life correctly. I say that because no matter how much advice I give you, you WILL make mistakes, you WILL experience grief, joy, sadness, happiness, loneliness, frustration, in fact every human emotion IF you are truly living. So be brave enough to put yourself out there and get amongst it, take the good with the bad. It's a cliché but 'life is not a dress rehearsal', so go and live it!

On that point, it's your life, not your parents' or siblings' or friends', yours! They, of course, are an incredibly important part of your life but should not define it. So listen to your heart. When you do things that give you joy, peace and satisfaction, keep doing them. The people who really love you will respect your choices, as long as they don't harm others or yourself, and should acknowledge your right to your own destiny. If they don't and try to block your path, gently and politely request that they move aside and support you in your passion. They may resist, but ultimately, if they can see that you are clear and committed to the path you are on, they should get behind you.

Now, I do not intend this advice to sound like you should become self-centred or self-obsessed. On the contrary, that would be a tragedy.

To counter the possibility of this and to give true depth and meaning to your life, you must develop an acute sense of compassion and service to others. Whilst pursuing your own goals you must take every opportunity to consider the welfare of others and do whatever is in your power to help and support them. You must also remain humble by giving back to society whenever the opportunity arises. It fills you with such a sense of purpose and belonging that it will make all other achievements all the more rich as they will have context. (You may not understand the concept of 'context' yet, but trust me it's important!)

If you see someone who needs help, ask if you can help. They may refuse but give them the option. Try not to live your life asking only 'What's in it for me?' There is so much more than you.

Finally, have FUN! Try not to lose the clown within. Laugh. Keep things light. This won't always be possible but I believe you have a choice each day as to whether you are happy or not. Choose happy.

OK, you can go back to cricket now.

Lots of love to you,

Erik

EVA
ORNER

Eva Orner is an Academy and Emmy Award-winning film producer and director. She grew up in Melbourne and is now based in Los Angeles. Her works include *Untold Desires, Taxi to the Dark Side, The Life and Work of Dr. Hunter S. Thompson* and *The Network*. Her latest film, *Chasing Asylum*, a critical look at Australia's offshore detention policies, premiered in April 2016. Her book about the making of the film, also called *Chasing Asylum*, was released in 2016 by HarperCollins.

Before we get serious, just a quick word of warning.

DO NOT get that haircut. At that really cool hair salon some of your friends went to. Where the stylist cut your hair unevenly, one side long and one side super short. DON'T DO IT. You will go home crying and your mum will 'even it out' and you will have a short bowl cut that makes you look like a ten-year-old boy for the next three months.

Now that's out of the way, let's get serious. It's all going to be OK. Even better than OK. Here are some things you need to know:

Be kind. If you see someone at school who looks like they are having a hard time, say 'hi'. Be nice. Be sweet. At worst you may make them feel a bit better. At best you may make a new friend.

Be interested in what's happening around you and in other people. The world is more interesting than just you.

Ask questions. Never be embarrassed to ask questions.

People will say, 'There are no stupid questions.' Well, there are. Plenty of them, but IT DOESN'T MATTER. Better to ask a stupid question than not to ask.

Be curious. School is great but educate yourself as well. Read a wide variety of books. Read the paper every day. You're old enough to do that now. It's good to start developing a sense of what is happening in the world.

If something is interesting to you, pursue it. Don't worry if your friends think it's uncool. This is your time to be adventurous and try things out.

Fun is really important so find things that make you happy. Whether it's music, cooking, dancing, singing, writing, being with friends. Make sure you have fun regularly and laugh a lot.

Don't feel you have to be part of a gang. Some people like being in groups, some people don't. Be authentic to what makes you feel good.

Don't be afraid to fail. You can't succeed all the time and if you don't try you'll never know. It's so much better to try, fail and learn than to sit on the sidelines and maybe regret not trying later.

Don't feel the need to be grown up till you are. Being a kid is fun and exciting. Stay being a kid as long as you can.

And, most importantly, don't be too hard on yourself. You are OK.

Xx eva

FIONA
SCOTT-
NORMAN

Fiona Scott-Norman was born in England and moved to Australia in the 1980s. She's a writer, satirist, broadcaster and columnist who contributes to *The Age*, *The Australian*, 774 ABC Radio and *The Big Issue*. She edited *Bully for Them*, published by Affirm Press in 2014, and has also had several comedy shows that have toured the country.

Dear Fiona,

Hello! Helloooo! Your older self here! Be a dear and put that book down for a moment. I know, I know, you're right in the middle of a good bit, but I'm worth the effort. For one thing, it's a letter, an actual letter, and I know you're not getting many of those while you're at boarding school. None, right? Awful. Well, this is just one of the things I want to talk to you about – Fiona to Fiona – from the perspective of a) being a grown-up now, and b) having finally asked Mum and Dad what the actual friggety hell was with them not writing to me at school.

(By the way, I swear a fair amount these days. It's tremendous fun being older. You'll love it.)

So. The reason you're not getting any letters from home has nothing to do with *you*. It turns out that Mum is self-conscious about writing letters because she makes spelling mistakes. Maybe a bit dyslexic. Who knew? She's worried about being judged, probably because Dad's super shouty. And you're so good at English, and Mum's very proud of that, so she kind of doesn't want you to know that she hasn't the foggiest when 'e' goes before 'i', etc. Crazy, huh? So, look, you're not going to get much mail for your entire seven years at boarding school, and I know that makes you feel very lonely, but it's not because you're not loved. You are loved so very much! Mum and Dad adore you, they're just English and don't know how to show emotion.

You will eventually teach both of them to hug.

And you know how when you ring home, and Dad answers the phone, and immediately says, 'I'll get your mother,' and puts the phone down and walks off? That's not because he doesn't want to talk to you.

It's because he doesn't like talking on the phone. To anyone. But gosh he loves you. He thinks you're the bee's knees. I agree it's hard to believe when his nicknames for you are 'long streak of misery' and 'eldest unmarried', but it's true. He just never stopped being angry after the Second World War. If you can manage it, cut him some slack; he's still having flashbacks to body parts and bombing raids.

You're going to be fine. You don't have to worry. Truly! Life will not suck like an abdominal leech indefinitely. There's nothing wrong with you. I know it doesn't feel like that. Your nickname is 'Spider', nearly everyone at school teases you, you're a foot taller than all the boys, and it's horrible being the most unpopular kid out of nearly 2000 students. Hanging around like limp lettuce on the edge of the dancefloor at school socials, and never being asked to dance.

(I found a photo of Andrew H a few days ago. I know he's the apotheosis of spunkhood to you right now, but trust me, he's a big spotty oik. You missed out on nothing.)

(Kevin B, however, was a sweetie. I suggest not defeating him that time you wrestle in the Fry House common room.)

But school will be over before you know it and, despite your fear, 'deeply unpopular' isn't your brand for life. It also transpires that your giraffe-like legs are a drawcard once you grow into them.

(You will always have difficulty buying shoes, because even 40 years later a size 12 is ridiculous. However, your feet and hands are proportionate now, and no one ever laughs at them.)

Being an outsider at school, burying yourself in books, and making jokes to deflect the meanness will turn you into a writer and comedian. Everyone in your dorm marries early and pursues a safe profession, which frankly is a fate which would drive you bonkers with boredom.

You, young lady, with your sharp tongue, hypersensitivity and smarts, are going to have an interesting life. I expect you'll roll your eyes at this, but you are quite the package.

You will have breasts (eventually, they are comely and popular). You will never get a tan. Because you're so awkward and visible, and attract unwelcome attention, you are supremely comfortable with being uncomfortable. This sounds terrible, but trust me it's a gold standard attribute for a writer and performer. You're going to have a long and powerful career as a theatre critic because your care factor about being highly visible and talked about is zero.

It is okay to not fit in. You try so hard to fit in, but you will not find your tribe at a middle-class English boarding school in the 1970s. F*** no. Shy and miserable as you are, you are already a boundary pusher.

You will become Australian. (You will still never get a tan.) The bolder you get, the happier you are. You will love well. Now, back to that book!

Love,

Fiona

P.S. In December 1980, invest 100 quid in Apple shares. Yes, Apple. They make computers. Don't ask questions, just do it.

GLEN
CHRISTIE

Glen Christie has been a facilitator with
the Reach Foundation for more than fifteen
years, where he has created workshops that
allow participants to feel safe to delve into
their personal story, and reflect on what it is
that they want in life and how to get there.
Glen also works as an associate producer for
MasterChef Australia.

Dear 13-year-old Glen,

I want to let you know first and foremost that you are a very funny and charismatic guy who doesn't need to worry so much about the fact that you are gay. You are going to learn that it is actually something that will teach you to have understanding for others who are different. It will also mean that you will end up having a relationship with yourself that you couldn't even imagine. One where you can say to yourself, 'I am a good person.' You can speak up for yourself, you can go for all the things you want in your life. The funny teeth you have that you never got braces on are something unique to you. So smile and laugh and don't give a crap that they are crooked.

The biggest lesson I can give you, though, is to listen. Stop and really listen to what others are saying to you. Take the time to care about what other people are thinking and feeling: it is not always about you. If you do this you'll find that others might just do the same for you.

Crying and being vulnerable are good. You are a sensitive little guy. Don't hide it, always let it out. You will find that the courage to be honest will be hard, but it will mean that you have been true to yourself. Keep watching Disney movies – in your heart you are a kid, never lose the kid.

When people tell you to get a stable job, ignore them. They want stability so they don't have to feel scared. Opportunity comes with risk.

Explore your body and appreciate it for all that it is. Because it is going to carry you through this life. Don't let anyone put it down and especially not yourself. You can be so cruel to yourself. It doesn't help. Don't ignore it either, though. Stop and listen. Get active and breathe.

Friends, family and love are the most important things in life. Shoot for the stars, but never forget those three things, because without them, the dream is empty.

GREG
CHAMPION

Greg Champion is a songwriter, guitarist and radio personality who was born in Benalla, Victoria. He is most recognised for his work as part of the Coodabeen Champions as a songwriter and guitarist. Greg often writes songs about both Aussie rules football and cricket, and he's a multi-awarded country/folk singer.

Hello and pleased to meet you, 13-yr-old self. :-)

The one dominant thing that I wish to say to you is: you know what? – I have no advice.

That is because: *I didn't learn anything particularly special* that will help your journey!

And that is because: you are on your journey – and you're already going about it the right way! *That* is the major thought that arrives, when asking myself what I can share with you.

And *that* is because I trust you to know what you're doing, instinctively. Looking back at you from here, I reckon you had it pretty well sorted, for the most part – definitely not all of it – even though you certainly didn't know that at the time.

There is not a lot you could have changed, or should have. 'The journey is the journey.' You're on it. It's so true that it's more about the journey than the destination – in many ways if not all. Just do what you're doing. Without necessarily knowing it, you, my former 13-yr-old self, are on the right path already.

'There are no mistakes.' 'Everything happens for a reason.' I dearly like those two aphorisms, looking back from here – 47 years later (!) What happens will happen; cruise; 'go with the flow'; don't waste any time planning, worrying, stressing about the future: 'you only have now'. These are all somewhat Buddhist concepts that I'm quoting. I have found them to be the best ones for your journey, 47 years on.

Would I change a thing? Any mistakes I regret? Barely. And if there are one, two or five things I wish I could go back and do differently, arguably it's pointless to wish that, AND obviously they can't be undone now anyway. Because the journey – was the journey ...

I don't know if it's useful for us to revisit that time, my 13-yr-old friend. Single parent Housing Trust home in a rough suburb, sponsored to private school [Pulteney Grammar, sister school of CGS], 12 months younger than the rest of your year, bullied a bit and, sadly, guilty of bullying a bit yourself. I do know that making the top sport teams earned you more esteem from others and consequently, more self-esteem. But the brainboxes who didn't fancy sport usually had sufficient self-esteem to start with anyway.

Whatever challenges you/we may have had – being bullied, crowded, small humble home, heavy parent and sibling conflict, distinct lack of success with the opposite sex – with hindsight it was a pretty charmed ride, eh?

You, my 13-yr-old self, and I can laugh now about how well things have gone; we certainly had no idea back then, did we, that things would go half as well as they have! You had no inkling of this fantastic adventure life became; *you* – are a lucky duck.

If you had known then what a joyful journey life would be, you would have been walking around with a huge, mysterious grin on your face as a 13-yr-old, eh!

Lovely to meet you again, my 13-yr-old pal. You are bringing tears of emotion to my eyes.

SIR GUSTAV
NOSSAL

Sir Gustav Nossal is a research biologist who has written seven books and more than 530 scientific articles. Nossal has served as president or chairman of many prominent organisations, including the Australian Academy of Science and the Council for Aboriginal Reconciliation. He was knighted in 1977, made a Companion of the Order of Australia in 1989 and has received honours from sixteen countries. In 2000 he was appointed Australian of the Year.

Dear teenage Gus Nossal,

I am sending you this letter from my 84-year-old self with a few bits of advice as you buckle down to your second year of secondary school in case these few bits of wisdom can smooth the path of your next few years.

First, strive to learn rather than to shine. I know how ambitious you are and how annoyed you get if anyone beats you in an exam, no matter how trivial. But school shouldn't be about coming first, it should be about learning, remembering and growing. What you cram for the exam goes in quickly, is forgotten just as quickly. When you learn the right way, reading beyond the immediate subject matter, enquiring of others their opinions in the area, this rounds you out as a person and forms part of your continuing upbringing.

Second, try to be a little less arrogant. I know often your arrogance is just part of showing off a bit, but it can be hurtful. OK, some people are not as bright as you, but they are people nevertheless, with feelings and sensitivities. Your thoughtlessness might hurt them much more than you think. Also, your parents don't like it when you dismiss the views of their friends as silly or superficial. Learn to be open to all views: some of them might be more valuable than you think.

Thirdly, try to be a bit less untidy. Your handwriting is shocking, if you would just slow down a bit, there would be fewer smudges and it wouldn't be so terribly hard to read. There's no need to go around with spots all over your school uniform, and remember your long socks are supposed to come up to just below your knees, not to slump around your ankles. And making your bed in the morning wouldn't hurt either. Gus, I know you are basically a good person, and life will gradually smooth off some of these rough edges, but being a bit less self-satisfied and a bit more conscious of the needs and desires of others will really help you. Good luck for your next few years, your final school examinations, and the university course that clearly lies ahead.

With best wishes

Your future self

Gus Nossal

GUY
SEBASTIAN

Guy Sebastian is a singer–songwriter and the first winner of *Australian Idol*. Guy was born in Malaysia in 1981 and moved with his family to Australia at the age of six. Over the course of his career, Guy has received 22 ARIA Award Nominations and has been part of *The X Factor*'s judging panel.

Dear Little Guy,

I realise that at your age you believe that you know everything about everything, but please believe me, you have a lot to learn. Firstly, and most importantly, this letter is not about asking you to change. Yes, your actions and attitudes are what define the outcomes of your life, however it's not about getting it all 'right'. You're going to make mistakes. Get over that. It's okay. Mistakes are the only way to learn.

Sometimes people will let you down. Sometimes you will let yourself down. Sometimes things won't go your way. Sometimes your heart will get broken. Here's the big one … Sometimes, actually often, your trust will be broken and people will take advantage of you. HOWEVER, don't ever let this change you. Don't let the negative things in your life shape your behavioural patterns and the way you interact with people. Remain trusting, loving and positive because there are people who love you and believe in you. If you let the bad experiences close you up, you won't be able to receive these things from the positive people.

All that time you're spending on music, keep doing it. People will tell you it's not a possibility, that you don't have the right 'look', that you're not good enough etc. They don't have a crystal ball.

University might seem like a hindrance from the dream; however, your degree will lead you to work with people much less fortunate than you and this will teach you invaluable lessons about appreciation.

With success comes temptation. Situations will present themselves that can alter the course of your life forever. Have some foresight and choose wisely. Try to discern the difference between what is fleeting and what is eternal. The latter will soothe your heart, the former only your physical needs. In other words, hold on to what matters with a tightly clenched fist.

Lastly, always put love first. Don't lose your love for people. It will be easy to at times. There are always multiple sides to every situation. Try to understand perspectives other than your own, because you are hard-headed and will often be wrong.

Guy

PS. Don't steal those lollies because Paul dared you to. You will get banned for life from Foodland.

JACKIE
FRENCH

Jackie French's writing career spans twenty-five years, thirty-six languages, more than 140 books and more than sixty awards in Australia and overseas. Her books include *Diary of a Wombat* and *Hitler's Daughter*. She was the Australian Children's Laureate for 2014–2015 and the 2015 Senior Australian of the Year.

Dear Jackie,

I can't tell you what comes next. If you fail to squish a caterpillar tomorrow on the oleanders its resultant butterfly may change the world by the flap of its wings and I might not be sitting here writing you this. (This is part of an exciting theory involving Mandelbrot sets but it hasn't been formulated yet in your time. But you'll have fun later with its implications.)

I *can* tell you that nearly all your dreams will come true. Not all of them – you must admit that starring in *La Traviata* at La Scala is not compatible with writing books on a headland surrounded by bush and owning a hundred dogs. Nor do your dreams come true in exactly the way you envisage. But then, you know extraordinarily little of the vast complexity of possibilities that is life. But if today you could choose where you'd be at 61, which is how old I am as I write this to you, I think you'd choose it all – every second of the life that has led you to here.

Which is not to say it has been easy. There will be bumps and some great slashes. But they will pass. They are also minuscule compared to all the good.

The years you are in now are the worst in your life: the most isolated, socially and intellectually, with no family comfort and your experiences too foreign to your friends for them to even accept what is happening to you, much less support you. Besides, you will learn, many, many decades later, your school friends too have hard walls to climb just now, and you too will have failed to support them.

But you must believe this: IT IS NOT YOUR FAULT. Nothing of

the past few years or now or the few years to come – is your fault. Despite what you now think and feel, you are still a child and it is the duty of others to protect you. Do not feel guilty, because for many years guilt tore or nibbled you. No matter how long our life will be, it will be too short to waste on guilt that you did not deserve.

Believe this too: you are lovable and will be loved, even if there is no one to love you now. Once you get to university you will find a growing network of people with minds that match your own. You will also find that similar minds were with you at school, all the time, but partly because you were focused, mostly, on surviving, but also because of the low intellectual expectations of girls back when you were thirteen, you won't see them.

Believe this, most of all: that no matter what hard things happen in your life, at the same time there will be happiness and beauty around you too. Mostly, you will find these yourself, but it's worth advising you to look a little harder for the glorious bits and enjoy them all the more, knowing that, yes, it's all okay. It works out. Time and again, all your life – until today, at least, and I hope for a long while still to come – it all works out.

What else? Forget those diagrams for that perpetual motion machine. It won't succeed. But don't narrow the breadth of your thinking either: you will have some major insights, though you will give them to specialists in the appropriate fields, which will not be yours, to refine and publish.

And maybe I need to tell you this too: the best that is yet to come is far beyond your daydreams, with a richness you could never have imagined. But the deepest joys have come from the mundane things that you are slightly scornful of now – as wife, mother, friend, part of the bush around you and a few other everyday fulfilments I won't spoil for you by foretelling them.

I wish I could comfort you now. I can't. But there is comfort and joy around you, even now, if you look.

Do look.

Love (even if it took me decades to be able to say this),

Jackie

JAMES
O'LOGHLIN

James O'Loghlin is one of Australia's most respected corporate speakers, corporate comedians and media personalities, best known as the host of more than 300 episodes of *The New Inventors* on ABC TV, and for his programs on ABC Local Radio. His novel for children, *The Adventures of Sir Roderick, the Not-Very Brave*, won the Speech Pathology Australia award for the best novel for 8 to 10 year olds.

James,

Listen. You spend way too much time worrying about what people think about you. You think that whatever you do is assessed and analysed, and that if you do anything silly, stupid, clumsy or awkward, they'll be onto you.

Guess what? No one is watching your every move. They really aren't. In fact, apart from your family, no one thinks about you much at all. I'll prove it. Think of someone in your class. How long do *you* spend thinking about *them* every day? Hardly any time at all, right? And that's how long they, and everyone else, spend thinking about you. They're all too busy thinking about themselves. And that's a good thing, because it means that you don't have to worry so much about trying to live up to their expectations.

So try to relax. In your teens you become self-conscious. You get scared of making a fool of yourself, but that fear can stop you having new experiences and throwing yourself into things. Whether it's footy or cricket or drama, you sometimes think that the safest thing is not to have a go at all because you're scared of looking stupid.

Have a go! Don't miss out. There's lots on offer, so jump into it. If you find you're no good at something, that's okay. You can either practise and get better at it, or try something else.

Remember this. Mostly, if someone is good at something, it just means they have done it a lot. With practice, you can get good at almost anything.

Try to *think* less and *do* more. When you catch yourself worrying about stuff, distract yourself. Read a book, talk to a friend, do some exercise, write, whatever. But don't sit there endlessly analysing yourself.

Hassle your parents to get you a guitar and either get lessons, or a book you can teach yourself from. Get a yoga book and do 20 minutes of yoga every day. Just do. It's good for everything – fitness, discipline and feeling good about yourself.

Do more sport. Don't worry about whether you're good at it, or whether you're going to get hurt, just stop thinking and throw yourself into it.

If something goes wrong or you do something stupid, don't panic. In a week no one will remember it. Even adults can't tell you what was on the front page of the paper a week ago.

To be honest, you're not going to really feel that you know what you should be doing until you discover stand-up comedy in about 11 years' time, so until then you might as well just be nice to people, do your homework, throw yourself into things and find as many things as you can that you enjoy.

And don't watch too much television! Seriously, you might think *Dallas* is good, but in 30 years *Breaking Bad* will blow your mind!

All the best,

Older James

JEN
CLOHER

Jen Cloher is a singer–songwriter currently based in Melbourne. Originally from Adelaide, Cloher moved to Sydney to pursue a degree at NIDA. In 2006 she released her debut album *Dead Wood Falls* as Jen Cloher & The Endless Sea, garnering an ARIA nomination for Best Female Artist. Her third album, *In Blood Memory*, was nominated for the Australian Music Prize in 2013.

Dear Twelve-Year-Old Me,

It's 1986, in Adelaide. An only child, you've spent most of your life at Loreto Ladies Convent, a rather stuffy Catholic girls' school. Your look would best be described as 'androgynous'. When not dressed in school uniform, you frequently get mistaken for a boy. In fact, you have a pinball-playing alter ego who passes at the local takeaway as John – until your mum walks in one day and yells, 'Jennifer! Come home at once!'

You're a colourful, creative individual, drawn to the arts like a magnet. You even get to play the lead role of Jesus in the end-of-year drama production. Desperate to fit in, you're a student representative for your class, head of the debating team and a consistent B-grade student. From the outside, things look okay.

But secretly you hate it there. There in the prison of scary old nuns, academic achievement and regulation blue underwear.

Don't worry – in a year's time everything will have changed. You'll have been expelled from Loreto, smoked your first bucket bong, and changed from ra-ra skirts and Duran Duran to twelve-hole Doc Martens and The Dead Kennedys. But, for now, let's address your current situation.

You are in love. Absolutely, positively besotted with Caroline Clark – a bronzed goddess with piercing blue eyes and perfect caramel curls that cascade effortlessly down her back. Caroline is the definition of 'natural beauty'. She's a country boarder at Loreto with exceptional athletic ability. Over the course of year eight you strike up a friendship, and when mid-term holidays arrive you spend them at her farm in

Mildura. Here you learn how to drive a car, go to your first bush dance, sleep out in a caravan and smoke Escort Reds. You long to kiss Caroline but know that such a move would be unwise – humiliating, even. And so you set in motion many years of unrequited crushes – your secret heart.

1986 is the year of Halley's Comet. The year, like the comet, is a bit of a fizzer. It's the year Farnsy releases his career-defining album *Whispering Jack*. But you're listening to The Boys Next Door. The girl responsible for this change in your musical palate is Danielle Henderson, a mousy, quiet, unassuming soul. She arrives at Loreto in a shroud of mystery. Rumours fly that she was expelled from her last school, although no one seems to know why. You are immediately drawn to her.

1986 is the year Richard Lowenstein releases *Dogs in Space* starring Michael Hutchence. But it's the soundtrack to the film that captivates you. This is your first life-changing long player and you listen to it every night. For the first time you hear Nick Cave singing Roland S Howard's timeless heartbreaker 'Shivers'. You also love Iggy Pop's 'The Endless Sea'. You think he's singing 'The Embassy' in reference to a secret spy agency, but he's actually talking about shooting smack. You'll use the song title to name your band eighteen years later. That's Jen Cloher & The Endless Sea, not The Embassy. Cheers, Iggy!

Danielle Henderson is just a friend. There's no chemistry. She's like the gateway drug to your teen rebellion and she opens the door to a brand new world. You meet her gothic pals, drink goon in Rundle Mall, listen to The Birthday Party and dream of somehow escaping the drab confines of your Catholic girls' school.

Thirteen is fast approaching and year nine will bring with it a whirlwind of change. You'll get into a lot of trouble at school and start a secret life your parents never really find out about.

It's scary now, looking back at the kind of danger you're about to put yourself in. At the same time, I thank you for breaking free, for being an individual, for not fitting in. That spirit will cause you a lot of problems in life but also keep you moving forward and taking risks.

I recently found out that your year eight crush, Caroline Clark, committed suicide last year, just weeks before she was to be married. It made me feel very sad. I wonder how she really felt at twelve years old? And what of Danielle Henderson, the inspiration to your teen rebellion? She's now a qualified nurse, married with two beautiful boys and living in Adelaide. I still see her from time to time for a cuppa and everything seems just fine.

In fact, Twelve-Year-Old Me, that's the main thing I want to tell you: don't worry, life will work itself out, you will fit in one day. Sure, it'll take another eighteen years of feeling like a square peg in a round hole, but you'll figure it out. Writing to you twenty-four years on, I wish I could somehow reach into your little heart, as a whisper from the future, and give you the confidence to put yourself out there. To pursue the ones you love rather than shrinking away in fear. To be a colourful creative and to trust you will make a living from it. I'd like to let you know you are already enough, that you don't have to be anything more for anyone else. That you are beautiful, even though you can't yet see it.

But if I wasn't you then, I wouldn't be me now. And that's all that matters: now.

JO
STANLEY

Jo Stanley is a TV and radio personality who grew up in Melbourne. She's currently host of *Jo & Lehmo* on GOLD104.3, and previously hosted *Weekend Breakfast* on the Hit Network and *The Matt and Jo Show* on Fox FM from 2003 until 2013.

Dear 13-year-old Jo,

Right now, you think the world has ended. Your best friend, Lina, has stopped talking to you for no reason and even though you've begged her to tell you why she just gives you the silent treatment and goes off with Amy at lunch and you're left on your own trying not to cry in the back of the library. I know. It is devastating. It's a baffling and bruising pain that you will remember at strange times over the next 30 years, and you'll be sad for that little girl who just wanted to be accepted and approved of and loved.

The great news is that while Lina will come around, you don't need her. Tania is your true BFF (QUICK, go spread that turn of phrase, you'll be the first by 10 years and be LEGENDARY!!). With Tania, you'll laugh like you've never laughed before, cry without shame, dance and sing and – well, I'll leave it up to you to live the next few decades hanging out with Tan. I'm envious you have that ahead of you. I'd relive it all in a heartbeat.

I must give you these little titbits, though, as a future version of you who has finally managed to get good hair (hang in there – it gets better).

First, it doesn't matter how you argue it, Andrew is not the cool one in Wham! Stop insisting on it. Possibly that's why Lina's gone cold (just saying).

Second, you and Simon Le Bon DO have a special connection. Right now, he's just a poster on your wall and the winner of your Spunkiest Hunk of 1985 Award. In about 23 years, you will interview him and he will look deep into your eyes and tell you that you're beautiful and it won't be a surprise because you knew it was meant to be.

Third, I know all you want in the whole wide world is a bubble skirt and your mum won't buy one for you and everyone in your year has one and you could just die from the shame of it. But here's a lesson that I wish wish WISH I had learned at your age, and not be still struggling to master now. You will never be happy if you compare yourself to other people.

You haven't had the easiest of starts in life. Your dad died, your mum has been sad and single and struggling to make ends meet. You feel lonely often and can't quite work out where you belong. The magical knowledge, though, is that everyone else feels this too. Everyone else has that voice in their head saying they're no good. Everyone else is hiding the same pain.

So stop focusing on what others seem to have that you don't. You have everything you need inside of you – kindness, humour, intelligence and tenacity. Allow those qualities to replace the self-doubt and fear that follow you everywhere you go. Be brave and curious. Laugh lots and listen carefully. Make the choices that are right for you, and always speak your mind. Make mistakes. Never forget, you alone are enough. And I love you.

With all of my heart,

43-year-old Jo

P.S. Just because I can, let me ease your mind: you *will* grow boobs, you *will* get a boyfriend, and yes, you *will* get a bubble skirt. You'll be 37 and it will be for an 80s bad taste party, but it's never too late for dreams to come true.

Josh Frydenberg is the Federal Member for Kooyong and the Minister for Resources, Energy and Northern Australia. He was born in Melbourne and attended high school there. He was elected to the Australian House of Representatives in 2010 and re-elected in 2013. He is the seventh person since Federation to hold his seat.

As a school student, I never thought I would be a politician.

My dream was to be a tennis player. Every weekend was spent on the court and at one stage I even wanted to leave school and compete on the tennis circuit full time.

Thank goodness my parents said 'no way' and encouraged me to finish school! It was the best decision I could have made. In the end, after finishing school, I did get my chance to play tennis full time for a year, after which I was ready for university and a career path that has led to Parliament.

Looking back on my journey, my advice to you is to enjoy every day and work hard at everything you do – because you tend to be good at what you work hard at and enjoy what you are good at.

Studying may sometimes seem a little boring but in the end it's very worthwhile. It's a stepping stone for opportunities later in life. But not everything revolves around school and the marks you may get. The key is to follow your passion and always dare to dream. You never know what is around the corner, but it is often an opportunity to do what you hope.

My other message is 'never give up'. In my own life experience, not everything has gone my own way. I remember running for school captain and losing the race. As I have said, I dreamed of being a professional tennis player but after a year on the circuit I knew I was probably not good enough to do it for the rest of my life. The first time I ran for Parliament I failed to win the Liberal Party selection. It hurt at the time but I learnt from the loss. I would not be defeated and the next time I put my name forward I won. The message is that persistence pays off and more often than not you will succeed on the second, third or fourth attempt – it doesn't matter.

To quote the Latin phrase *carpe diem*, seize the day!

Best wishes and good luck,

The Hon Josh Frydenberg

JUDITH
LUCY

Judith Lucy, born and raised in Perth, is a comedian best known for her stand-up work. She's also the bestselling author of two books and created two ABC series: *Judith Lucy's Spiritual Journey* and *Judith Lucy Is All Woman*. Judith is also the 2015 winner of the Helpmann Award for Best Comedy Performer.

I know at the moment that things are pretty grim.

Your parents fight all the time, you're still trying to work out what the hell sex is, you know nothing about boys, and your best friend is horrible. To add to this, a girl called Mandy, who is a year older, has started bullying you. Generally she just hassles you about having curly hair but you're convinced that she wants to do some damage to you with a Bunsen burner. Every time you see her in the corridor you're terrified. Lastly, you love performing, but everyone (especially your parents) tells you that while that might be a lovely hobby, you'll never make a living out of it. Your father is very keen for you to be an accountant.

One of the worst things about being thirteen is that you're so close to being an adult, you can almost taste it ... but you're not and sometimes it's hard to imagine even making it to eighteen.

The good news is that I'm writing you this letter at forty-seven, so you survive it all. In fact, you're pretty happy with yourself. The bad news is that you do a lot of stupid things before you get here. I would tell you more about that but I don't want to take the fun out of being so drunk on a flight once that you and your best friend had no memory of getting off the plane apart from the fact that you knew it involved security guards and wheelchairs. Anyway ... that's all ahead of you and, like most people, you survive your twenties.

Let's take your problems one at a time. Unfortunately, your parents will keep arguing, but, and I know this currently seems about as likely as a Kardashian becoming a philosopher, they ultimately make peace with each other and wind up being closer than you've ever seen them. They even go away on holidays together. (Which admittedly you and your brother resent because they never took you anywhere apart from the one time you all went away and never got out of the car. I mean NEVER. It was like the family was on a plane – that's okay too, though, because this resentment actually leads you to write a few pretty good jokes about them.)

I'm not going to sugar-coat the next bit; it takes you years to work out sex and boys. You even wind up going home with a man who thinks that you're a transvestite (yes, you most certainly do write a routine about this ... have you guessed what you wind up doing for a living yet?) but you wind up with some very nice boyfriends and the one you have now is a real keeper.

You're very close to finding a new best friend, Michelle, which is really good news. You're still friends with her and her whole family thirty years later and some of your best memories from this time involve her. You have a bad patch in your twenties when one of her Communist friends urinates on your carpet, but the friendship endures.

As for Mandy, you bump into her years later in a mall and she acts like the two of you were always best friends ... you feel sorry for her, especially because she still has blonde streaks and hair the size of a Shetland pony.

One of the most deeply, deeply irritating things about life is that clichés really are clichés because they're true. You do learn from failure and time really does seem to heal a lot of wounds. Even more annoyingly, hard work does generally pay off. I wish I could tell you that you will learn everything you need to know and have every emotional scar patched up by watching *Friday Night Lights* (you haven't seen this show about high school gridiron players yet but you will LOVE it) and that your dreams will come true if you just sit on the couch and eat a lot of sausage rolls, but it doesn't seem to work that way.

What I'm trying to say is that you get over the anger that you have for your parents and wind up loving and understanding them so much more as you get older, you let go of the resentments you have about people treating you badly because you get better at treating yourself well and come to understand that the Mandys of this world can't be having a very nice time either … and that it's worse for them because they are stuck inside their own heads. And by working very hard at performing (and failing a lot – why do you go on stage wearing nothing but a garbage bag and pointy rubber ears one night?) you wind up becoming a professional comedian and making even Ann and Tony Lucy proud.

You actually start to work some of this stuff out around about now and, even though it might be hard to imagine, you'll look back at this time fondly … at the very least, you'll look back and laugh.

JULIAN McMAHON

Julian McMahon is a Melbourne barrister who has been the lawyer for Van Tuong Nguyen and members of the Bali Nine. Julian has been named Victorian Australian of the Year for his work as a barrister and advocate for human rights.

Dear Julian,

Two months ago, I was asked to write this letter of advice to you, trying to use my own experience as something positive. That has turned out to be harder than it sounds because life at your age was messy. On the surface, you functioned well enough, but the usually dramatic and confused life happening inside you seemed so different from what was happening around you.

You were feeling hemmed in, jammed, that life was all pretty messy and confusing. You were feeling that it's so hard to have intense feelings such as love, hate, fear, and dreams of adventures which you can't really discuss or share, that it's so hard to want something entirely different in your day but knowing it's just not going to happen. So, what can I say that is useful?

My first main point: whatever is happening now, it passes. From all these years later, I see now that good days and bad, worries, passions, disappointments, rages, excitements, they all pass. Of course, everything that happens in our lives shapes us, but that is a different discussion.

Life changes a lot, no matter what you do. Each phase of life brings a whole new range of things which are significant. Think back to when you were seven and what mattered then. So if life at 13 is mostly hard not easy, don't fret. That's a very good reason to stop being harsh on yourself, by the way. If you've made bad mistakes, don't repeat them, learn and move on.

Let me offer another point to consider: hope is central to life. Spend time on it – it can be liberating and guiding. As a small example, you'll begin to plan some travel adventures, and then by the time you're leaving school, you'll begin to do them. You get to an age and state of freedom where you can sometimes actually plan and do things. That can be a lot of fun.

Have I got any advice? Yes. It is to try to think long-term. If you can really get a sense of a bigger world, a far-off horizon, then start planning for it – what you read, watch, dream, discuss. If you have to do much of it alone, so be it. Planning, hoping, seeing the present for what it is – to be lived well, knowing it is passing. These things help you through the ugly stuff, and help you shape where you are going, what you do, what sort of life you lead, how you affect the world, how you let the world affect you. Please repeat those last seven words.

I have found it hard to confine this letter to how to deal with a tough few months at 13. I find myself thinking about your whole life, not just at 13. Maybe the two ideas can hardly be separated. How do you have the happiest life possible, real and profound happiness, whatever age you are?

I'm pretty sure that a lot of the happiness in life is about finding a balance between at least these three things: being as generous as possible, realising your plans and dreams (courage), and taking the time to learn things well (hard work). Maybe the balance or weight shifts between these if you are burdened with illness or frailty. So be it. Somewhere in that combination is also freedom – your choices, not someone else's choices for you. Your choices will be right for you, make more sense, if you are having courage, being generous etc.

I can't say for sure why being generous is so important – and I most certainly don't think anyone should be a doormat – but I can say for sure that I don't know any happy people who are not generous. Also, I don't know anyone who is not generous but who is happy. But for some, life is hard and I do know some people who are generous but fate won't let them find much happiness. At your age, being generous probably means looking after family, other kids (who are maybe pretty messy like I was!) lonely neighbours, needy people. Whatever it takes, do it. Be generous in the little things.

As I have tried to write this letter, so many issues have come to mind. Should I try to talk to you about how to make friends, how to deal with dishonesty, cruelty, bullying, how to manage selfish people who can make this time of your life miserable? Or about relationships, about the confusion you might feel with so much that is happening around you, about feeling clueless concerning the future, about the sense of missing out on things, be it friendship, love, cool clothes, whatever? All of those ideas could make a chapter.

But I can't write about all those things here and now. What I can say is that the world you are now in will soon be different and other worlds will come your way. And with that in mind, you can approach all these issues with the three ideas I put above.

I have to tell you – one thing you learn as you get older is that life is usually messy, no matter your age. It's not like you get to a point where all is well and clear, and then you start living. Rather, we just live in and out of different kinds of mess and do our best to make it worthwhile, no matter how simple or complicated our life and work are. Sometimes it's easy, sometimes hard. And while we do it, we try to be happy, make others happy, make the world a better place. That is a life worth doing. For most of us, in all that mess you can find some truly great happiness. In my opinion, this is true whether you are at work, school, home, travelling, whatever. In a sense, every part of life has permanence. It has happened and won't be undone. But change is always happening too.

Your plans, your courage, your dreams, doing these well, being generous (which brings you and others dignity, by the way), learning – all these will let you have a lot of say in which direction you go. The mess around you now will count for very little.

And because I am an old bore I have to say this as well – you have an education and access to books. So ... the hardships we find at 13 in our lives are, for most of us, even if truly intense, nevertheless pretty small compared to the hardships of kids who never have an education, a book, a safe home, a safe day. That's not our fault, and at some point we can – must – all do something about those problems, but when life seems too unpleasantly messy, we all need to keep perspective, all through our lives, at 13 and 52.

JUSTIN
HEAZLEWOOD

Justin Heazlewood (aka the Bedroom Philosopher) is a Tasmanian-born songwriter, author and actor who lives in Melbourne. Most known for his writing and musical comedy works, he has released several albums, performed at many arts festivals, been nominated for an ARIA Award, published several books about the entertainment industry (including *Funemployed*, Affirm Press 2014) and is a regular guest on several Australian radio shows.

Dear Justin,

THINK QUICK – BEHIND YOU!

In fifteen seconds a bully is going to try and dack you. This is the single moment which will define the rest of your life at Parklands High School. I'm writing this letter to see if I can stop the cycle of pants being pulled down. Legend has it that everyone in the Heazlewood family was dacked on the first day of high school (undies and everything!).

Okay, if this letter gets to you too late – that's okay. You will have been dacked by now and probably most of the school will have seen your bum and doodle. I reckon once you've been dacked you've got nothing to lose anyway, so you may as well play it for laughs. Jump up and down, waddle around. It's cool. It's like a metaphor for life. (You'll learn about metaphors in Miss Stones' English class – can you be honest with her about her breath, please?)

What I'm saying is: if life pulls down your pants, then pull up your socks. Try not to get angry or upset – that's what the bullies want. Give them a smile and maintain your composure.

WARNING – IN FIVE MINUTES A BULLY WILL THROW AN APPLE CORE AT YOUR GROIN. WEAR A CRICKET PROTECTOR.

Okay, you're on your own now. I don't want to tell you too much because I don't believe in corrupting the space-time continuum, and because I love the person we are today. I'm afraid you'll have to go through all kinds of crap for the sake of 'character building'. That said, can you do the following?

1. Never buy any basketball cards. Instead, put the money in a

savings account. (Seriously, I need to pay rent this month and you don't even play or like basketball.)

2. Eat less sugar, that's why you get pimples.

3. The sooner you get contact lenses, the sooner girls will like you.

Here's a good tip. Everyone's got the same insecurities as you. That is actually the name of a song we write in 2002, so I think it's okay that I tell you. I mean, what are we going to do? Sue ourselves for plagiarising our own idea? (That's sort of a good metaphor for life as an artist anyway – haha, sorry mate, private joke.)

No, this is important. (CORE INCOMING!) High school is going to make you feel small and embarrassing and like all the other taller kids with better shoes and good face days have more of an idea how to live life – but the secret, and I KNOW THIS FOR CERTAIN – is that every single person, even the teachers, is secretly scared that no one will like them. So basically, no one has it any better than you – we're all pretty equal inside our own heads.

Not that it'll help you much because you have the THICKEST GLASSES IN THE WORLD. But at least you can save time worrying what people think about you – they're mostly worried about themselves. Also, your 'coke bottles' will impress the rest of the school, so let the tough grade tens try them on. Maybe charge 20 cents a go and then keep that money in your Dollarmites account so I can pay rent. It's okay to cry (just not at school or in public or around anyone you've ever met, including the cats).

I love you. Kick arse – we're hilarious.

From your older self. Melbourne, 2015. (I'm in the future – we have phones like Penny's 'computer book' in *Inspector Gadget*. Carlton is shit, though. Sorry.)

KATE
CEBERANO

Kate Ceberano AM is a Melbourne-born singer whose solo album *Brave* earned her a 1989 ARIA Award for Best Female Artist. A year later, she won another ARIA for Best Female Artist, as well as one for Highest Selling Single. Her achievements now include five platinum albums, five gold albums and more than 1.5 million albums sold in Australia alone.

Dear Kate,

How's it going? How are you dealing with all the savage changes that are occurring to your body and to the world around you? It's kinda tough, yes? I know!

And there is so much I can tell you but I'm afraid you will probably continue to do it the way you will do it, because that is the way you have always gone about doing things. You will rarely repeat the same mistake twice, but you will make mistakes. But, you will learn from these mistakes ... painful mistakes, embarrassing mistakes and sometimes heartbreaking mistakes, but you'd rather make them than be warned off them. It seems to be a part of your character.

This character trait is both beautiful and brave, and yet will be frustrating to you and the people who love you.

So, I will go against nature and tell you a few things to avoid, and hopefully you will listen and change your mind, and avert some dangers that lie ahead.

You will be choosing one of the most dangerous industries, fraught with emotional blackmail, greed, materialism and double values. It attracts villains and good guys alike ... they are all attracted by the attention that you can create. It's like a bankable currency that those who love money and pretty things can't help but fall in love with. They will seek to own you, alter you and influence you, and you must resist. They will appear to know more than you and will tell you so in order to control your choices. But that is what you have that is Golden and must be protected at all cost. Choice!!!!!!

You can motivate the world around you by making strong,

meaningful choices. Choices that lead you toward the greater good of those around you. So when you become a leader (and you will be one in many areas of your life) in your band, or helping others on a community council, or when you become a festival director or even when you're singing in the chorus in ensemble ... no matter how big or small, your choice is your choice and is more important than responsibility. I say that because to be responsible sometimes can feel anti-intuitive, especially when you are obliged to be responsible. If you CHOOSE to be responsible then that is the higher path.

Because the artist has only her choice. And it defines her actions above all others. It's what makes her talent ignite and consequently affect the world around her. Good and bad.

It's the fragile flower that blooms only when it is admired ... by you!

And if your choices are compromised you may lose confidence in yourself and perhaps, from time to time, wish that you were someone else. You may get sad and compare yourself to others and come up short. You may decide to be influenced and follow others and discover that you no longer know your own mind. And forget that you ever had a choice.

But you do! And you always will.

Be brave and know that you inherited a kindness (from Grandma Kath) that is innate to you and your wish to be liked by others is actually a nice quality.

You seek to serve and your pay for helping others is to feel included. There is no crime in desiring this, but know this much ... Not everyone will like you and it will hurt. Life has many different types of people and some simply reject kindness like a knee-jerk reaction. Some instinctively distrust kindness and consider that it has something unknown behind it. But as your daughter says (and, yes, you will have a beautiful girl full of kindness and grace), all people are good but some are trained badly! This is a very wise statement. You cannot alter the fact that some people will endure all kinds of unkindness before they meet or work with you, and for them it will be synonymous with pain.

This all seems very heavy, I know, but you must be warned and try not to be liked by such people. You will break your heart trying.

On the upshot ... you have a most amazing career ahead of you, full of travel, full of love and music. And you will touch people with your song and bring comfort to many.

You are your own person; lead by example and never stop trying to improve yourself and the world around you. If you keep at it, you may even leave a path for others to follow.

Grace is eternal! Live a graceful life ... and have FUN!!!!!!!

Love you.

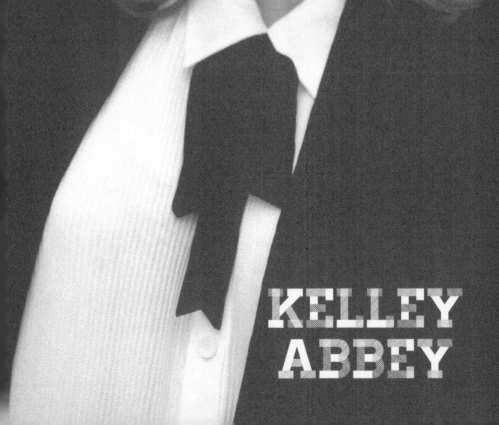

KELLEY
ABBEY

Kelley Abbey is a Brisbane-born actress, singer, dancer, choreographer and director. She has been a leading performer and choreographer in TV, film and musical theatre for more than 30 years. Kelley has worked on productions such as *So You Think You Can Dance* and the Oscar-winning film *Happy Feet*.

At 13 I was a shy kid just starting out at Corinda State High School in Brisbane. I was leaving Inala Primary and embarking on what I considered to be a foreign and scary environment on all levels. I must point out that I started dancing when I was 3 and had found an undeniable passion for the art of dance. The dance was where I got to escape. Where I got to be me. I was attending my dancing school and had made many great friends in my dance community. I had a real sense of belonging which is something that I never quite found at school. I also joined the Australian Youth Ballet Company when I was 12. In this semi-professional company I toured doing shows throughout Australia and also the UK. My schedule was very intense and even though I did well at school I almost felt I was living a double life. At dancing I was shy, but strong, powerful and felt beautiful. At school I felt self-conscious, not good enough and not pretty enough. I felt isolated and lonely. On the last day of high school I set my school shoes and uniform on fire. It was indicative of how I felt.

To my teenage self:

I wish I could travel back in time and hold you and tell you that you were beautiful, intelligent, artistic and worthy. I know you felt isolated at school. I know you felt like you didn't fit in. I'd tell you that people didn't embrace you as they were insecure and jealous. You had found your passion whereas others didn't even know what they liked.

Their snide comments and verbal and physical abuse came from jealousy. Teenagers can be so cruel. I feel your pain at being beaten up by girls and having had fruit thrown at your head on the school bus. I know this abuse left you not feeling good enough and ostracised. I know you were drowning in your new environment at high school. I know you were trying to make new friends, and coping with an ever-expanding amount of homework to juggle along with all of your dance life commitments. I recognise that you felt not attractive as you considered boys for the first time. I recognise the peer pressure from other kids to fit in or be initiated as 'cool'. Puberty blues seemed insurmountable. I know you missed a lot of school as you were performing. I know you loved it this way. You'd try and catch up and excel in your work, and this was a pressure in itself but you wouldn't have had it any other way. Little Kell, I would tell you that you did really well. You juggled a lot which is a skill that you will use in the future in the many roles you will play in your creative career. You were threatening to others because of your already awakened passion for dance and your internal power. Unbeknownst to you, you would grow and make the dance into a successful and satisfying career. You are also attractive and worthy ... Which will take you a while to find out but eventually you will. Everyone has their own tempo and timing in life. They say comparison is the thief of joy and this is absolutely true. You don't need to compare yourself with anyone else. Little Kell, you are safe and it is safe to be your authentic self: the beautiful dancing girl.

KEVAN
GOSPER

Richard Kevan Gosper AO is a Sydney-born former athlete who mainly competed in 400-metre events. He was also formerly a vice president of the International Olympic Committee. Kevan competed for Australia in the 1956 Melbourne Summer Olympics where he won the silver medal in the 4x400-metre relay with his team mates.

Thirteen is a significant milestone in age because it signals your entry to the teens.

It's also a significant time in your growth cycle in that many normal body functions, some externally obvious like changes in height, weight and hair – and, apart from this but more particularly, many changes that are taking place in your natural chemistry and internal bodily functions – all combine to sometimes raise uncertainties in your mind.

In the process of moving from childhood you are looking to take more responsibility for yourself, but on the other hand, parental, sibling and peer pressures seem to be louder and more obtrusive. Everyone seems to be offering you advice from the moment you wake up in the morning, off to school spending days in the hands of your teachers and when you return home. Of course you are also a new boy in a big school, and the senior students and prefects can seem something of a threat. I would suggest that you focus on your school environment, which takes up most of your waking hours, and seek out one or two friends who appear to have similar interests to yourself. Try to be socially responsive without overdoing it. Don't hesitate to seek advice and take it if it makes sense, but don't be too anxious to please. At all times be yourself. If you run into a serious problem be prepared to talk it over with your friends, your teachers or, of course, your parents.

High school is a great time of your life. You, in fact, have more freedom to make decisions about yourself than you realise.

Through your schoolwork and studies, look for subject matter that really appeals to you because you will do best in life applying yourself to the issues you favour. Finding out for yourself what you like to do, and to do it well builds your self-confidence and self-esteem, not only through your early teen years, but again later in life.

There is a lot of good in the world but 'nothing is perfect and nothing stays the same'. You will run into difficulties and problems with people and issues, but confront these and look for a solution earlier rather than later, otherwise you will become anxious and 'anxiety is a waste of time'. You should see these issues as small or large storms, but remember 'storms come and go, even big storms come and go'.

Most of all, keep your mind open to opportunities. There is so much ahead of you and there are always people who will come to your aid and act as mentors.

Finally, never forget that your family is the most important source for love and advice in your life.

LAYNE
BEACHLEY

Layne Beachley AO is a seven-time Women's World Champion surfer from Sydney. A 2006 Surfers' Hall of Fame inductee and a 2011 Sport Australia Hall of Fame inductee, Layne created the Layne Beachley Foundation 'Aim for the Stars' in 2003 to enable young girls and women across Australia to invest in their future and fulfil their potential.

If I had the opportunity to go back in time and give my teenage self some poignant words of advice, what would they be?

'Lighten Up!' Life is too short to take yourself seriously, so be kinder to yourself and those that you love. Comparing yourself to others only makes you feel inadequate, so appreciate others, learn from other people's mistakes and never put them on a pedestal. Placing them on pedestals or in pits prevents you from placing them in your heart. We all just want to be loved and accepted, even the bullies!

Being my own world's worst critic, with high expectations, I constantly made the mistake of projecting these expectations onto others. Fortunately, the guidance, love, support and patience of my friends and family help me to focus on the important things and keep my life in perspective by choosing to stop wasting my time worrying about everything out of my control.

'You can only control the controllable.' Honestly, the only things we can actually control are the thoughts we have. How often are you truly aware of what you think and how these thoughts affect your life in both a negative and positive way? Where do you place your focus? Do you think about what you *don't* want more than what you *do* want? I want to be happy. I want to belong. I want to be loved. I want to be accepted. Knowing these things enabled me to take actions towards achieving these outcomes and my dream of becoming a world champion.

Thought is expansive. What you think about, you create. The more you think about it, the faster you manifest it. Ultimately you are completely responsible for your current reality, and the sooner you learn to accept accountability for how you think and feel, the faster you will be able to create the life you truly want.

When you are feeling sad, scared, anxious or alone, have the courage to reach out to friends and family. People who support you, love you, believe in you and are willing to listen without criticism or judgement. These are the honesty barometers in your life and they will be your friends and mentors forever. There are too many critics and naysayers in the world who are dream thieves and life vampires. Deprive them of oxygen! The worst thing you can do when times are tough is to run and hide because that only prolongs the pain, suffering and despair.

The ocean is where I feel completely relaxed, nurtured and connected, so spend as much time in the water as you possibly can. Surfing enables you to reconnect with your true self. How do you maintain perspective? By spending time with quality friends, and sharing fears and concerns when they arise.

Find what makes you happy and commit to making the time for that activity every day. No one can make you happy but yourself! The quality of the questions you ask, the quality of people you hang around with and the quality of choices you make determine the quality of your life.

Always believe you are deserving of love and you are enough, just the way you are. Set Your Goals, Live Your Dreams and Never Give Up.

LISA
MAZA

Lisa Maza (Meriam/Yidindji/Dutch) has worked from Melbourne as a professional singer, actor and MC for the past sixteen years. In 2007, she began co-writing with her sister, and their autographically inspired theatre show *Sisters of Gelam* premiered at the Malthouse Theatre in November 2009.

Lisa, Lisa, Lisa,

I know high school isn't anything like what you imagined ... well, if truth be told, you hadn't really thought much about school after you left. When you found out you got into the high school everybody wanted to go to, you were excited but you soon got busy enjoying your holidays, and fair enough. There was winning Monopoly (beating Rachael), figuring out how many lollies you could get with the handful of coins you had or how cute the boy next door's friend was.

With the holidays well and truly over, you turn twelve and high school starts. Every day you go from classroom to classroom. Like a sheep you are herded along with the flock from one paddock to the next. You hate being treated like everyone else. A year goes by, you are thirteen and year eight begins. The rebellion starts. You assert your difference, your individuality. You begin by disregarding the uniform bit by bit: different-coloured stockings, ribbons, shoes, jumpers, much to the Maths master's disgust and the headmistress's disdain.

You put up with it in year seven but now you really hate teachers telling you what to do. Even your own (hippy) parents didn't boss you around. What gives teachers the right?

Newsflash! Teachers are there to teach, instruct ... I know you don't want to be bossed around, but trying to teach a class of thirty or more students requires some disciplining, particularly to those who continue to talk and distract others. And another thing for you to consider ... Teachers are human beings!!! I know ... it's shocking! When it dawned on me years after I left school, I was more than a bit surprised ... Oh, another thing ... they have feelings too. I know, it's a lot to absorb at your age ... but you need to know that talking in class makes their job very difficult and distracts them from doing what they are there to do. (Seriously, just put yourself in their shoes for one minute. Just give it a try, please!)

I know, I know, you need to express your teenage angst, but do you think putting thumbtacks on a teacher's chair is an appropriate way of punishing her for saying that 'you should be more like your sister' (who is at the same high school now and is apparently very well behaved, gets good results and listens in class). Look, to be honest your antics just waste everyone's time: the teachers, the students and, possibly even more importantly, yours! Most teachers are actually good people, who are genuinely interested in children getting a decent education and having a prosperous future.

I know, it seems like you've been in school forever already but this is the basis for the rest of your life. You do not want to waste the next six years of high school only to look back and regret that you could have learned so much, had an understanding of politics or been fluent in a foreign language (which would have been very handy when you travelled to Spain that time and were stranded after getting off a cheap Ryanair flight in the middle of nowhere – because you didn't even know the word for 'train', you couldn't even ask how to get the train to Barcelona) or discovered the history of the world, or had a grasp of geography, or commerce or many other useful things.

Being different doesn't mean being dumb, you know? Why don't you make being different mean being smart ... now that would really be something different!

Look, I've been around for 35 years longer than you and know a few things about you. You are a good person, you like people and people generally like you, you love cooking and eating and you adore adventure. You are smart but you just hate being told what to do. I've got some advice, which might be helpful. But you can obviously take it ... or leave it. It's up to you ...

This is your life. Enjoy and appreciate every moment of it because there is only one and it is happening right here, right now!!! It is not a dress rehearsal, this is it!!! Time is disappearing even as you read this, so hurry up and finish reading so you can get on with it.

If you want an exciting life, then try as many things as you can, as often as you can. Do, see, taste, listen, travel, dance, laugh and experience everything. Don't waste your time waiting for something to happen ... Make it happen!!!

Doing something is always better than doing nothing (except reading trash magazines, they will only make you feel ugly and are a waste of time). So work hard and don't be afraid to have a go. By having a go, you will at least figure out whether it is something you don't want to do, thus narrowing down your options in the future.

Don't worry about the future or what you want to do. I still don't know what I want to do ... and I'm a lot older than you. Opportunities will continue to present themselves to you throughout your life. You will take them ... or you won't.

Never worry yourself about what others say about you. It honestly says more about them than it does about you. Let it be water off a duck's back. You will only ever believe what you choose to believe anyway ... I can prove it: for example, if someone called you fat, dumb and ugly and someone else called you smart, talented and beautiful, which one would you believe, the first negative one or the second positive one? I suggest you take them both with a grain of salt or not at all. They are just someone else's opinion and they only become yours if you choose to believe them. Create positivity for yourself and in everything around you, because being negative will stop you from enjoying every wonderful possibility and fabulous experience in your life.

Stop blaming others! You are in control of your own destiny, and the sooner you realise this, the sooner you can get on with whatever it is you want to get on with.

Don't worry about what everyone else is doing. You can't control that. Just focus on what you're doing, because that is something you can control. The only race you need to be in is the one you set for yourself.

Make mistakes and make lots of them. This is what the journey of life is all about. Without mistakes we have nothing to learn from. Don't stress about the end results, they will come soon enough.

Forgive others and forgive yourself. Forgiveness is not about saying that someone is right (especially when you think they are wrong). It's about freeing you from the negativity of the past (the past being the past 10 years, 10 weeks or even 10 seconds) that will burden and distract you from wonderful life experiences in the future.

Love your family. Something wise Mum said is, 'Friends come and go but your family will always be your family.' It is true, they are here to stay (whether you like it or not) and I've come to believe that a family ends up together on this earth to learn something from each other. No matter how hard or easy that may be, you will know your family longer than anyone else in your life. Cherish them and let them know how much you love them, even if it seems a bit weird to do so.

Beware and be aware of fear. It is your worst enemy. Yes, fear is a natural thing and is very useful in the right circumstances; for example, if you are in physical danger. But that's not the fear I'm talking about.

Fear of failure, fear of success, fear of being seen to be trying too hard, fear of what others might think, fear that isn't real, that is not really threatening but appears that way in our head. That fear will never go away so don't waste time hoping it will. The best thing to do is to reduce its impact. Start by acknowledging it so you can continue forward and move beyond it. Don't let fear stop you from doing whatever it is you want to do or from expressing yourself fully. Be curious, excited, hungry, noisy, big and energised, and trust that everything will be okay, because it will.

You are your own worst enemy. Stop being so serious and critical, and start congratulating yourself for your achievements and appreciate who you are.

I would like to make a Toast ... To Love, Generosity and Courage!!!

LISA
MITCHELL

Lisa Mitchell is an English-born singer–
songwriter who grew up in Albury, New South
Wales. She rose to fame in the 2006 *Australian
Idol*. Her debut extended EP, *Said One to the
Other*, topped iTunes in Australia. Lisa relocated
to the United Kingdom where she recorded her
debut studio album, *Wonder*, which peaked
at No. 6 on the ARIA Chart and won the 2009
Australian Music Prize.

Hey Lise,

So you're 13, a really cool age! This will be a fun year; high school is a whole new world of learning about everything, playing more music and writing more songs, and navigating new friends and social circles. You're not very cool and you don't look like Summer from *The O.C.*, but hey, you're talented and smart and that will be cool in a few years, don't worry! You'll work out all that social stuff soon. You'll also get your period, which is the beginning of the next stage of your life; becoming a woman! Savour these young and carefree days! Go for big adventures with your sister on the farm, deep into the bush, and pretend you can live out there forever ...! Nature is still a huge part of your life and always will be. Be grateful for those trips to the white sunny ski-fields in Falls Creek and enjoy zipping through the cross-country runs ...! You are playing a LOT of soccer! You love being part of the team ... You are a hard worker at school but make sure you savour those moments in art class and really let yourself experiment and let go. What you learn and observe in art class will help you let go and create in other ways, like songwriting as well ... Be brave and make that girl-band! Rehearse in the ad breaks of your favourite TV show in the living room, and be silly and crazy if you want to be! Make sure you give yourself time alone at home to digest everything that's going on around you. You are really concerned about being individual and unique and you want to stand for something but you don't know what ... You are shy and quiet but you know you have a lot to say but you don't know quite how ... This is totally normal; write in your journal and sing and draw and make up songs to help you establish who you are and what you think and what you care about. Listen to yourself, and observe what you are drawn to in bookstores and the library and on TV ... Maybe there are some patterns ... Be the detective ... Perhaps you see Missy Higgins singing 'Scar' on *RAGE* and feel a very overwhelming bubbly fizzy infinite feeling in your body and think, 'I think I could do that ... I think I want to do that ...!' What I most want to tell you is that you are beautiful and not shy at all, just a dark horse waiting to bloom.

x endless love, past self!

Lisa (written from a hotel bed in London, June 2015)

Maggie Beer is a cook, food author, restaurateur and food manufacturer originally from Sydney. She has written nine books and appeared in many TV programs, including *MasterChef Australia* and her own show, *The Cook and the Chef*. Maggie's gourmet products are loved around Australia.

Well, Margaret Anne,

There might be 13 Margarets in your class so your surname is the identifying handle but I wouldn't worry about that and I can assure you that you'll find a derivative of 'Margaret' that suits you well, and years later you'll make it official by deed poll. Of the things I want to say to you, the thing that is most important in life is searching for what will give you happiness. It's a long journey and I want you to take courage that not fitting in actually gives you more strength and resilience than you can imagine right now. When you are lonely, books will be your friends but there is so much more you could do. You learn so easily if you're interested but you don't have the discipline of study. Think of what you could do with that extra edge, and even though you don't like physics and chemistry, find another way into the subject if you don't connect with your teacher, as everything you learn opens your mind to more exciting threads of knowledge. In the future there will be a revolution in learning in the internet that will link you into an unthinkable amount of knowledge; how exciting this is.

You might be a loner at heart but connections are vital and you need to search for them. Find a sport you love and be part of a team, a group, and have a go. The exhilaration of physical activity is real but it's best of all when there is an element of fun. Don't feel you have to be brilliant at everything so don't have a fear of failure, try as many things as you can. Never stop searching for what engages you. Experiences are like pieces of a jigsaw puzzle: one day they will all come together. Travel is a wonderful way of expanding your experience, your mind and finding new friendships. Travel will give you joy but along the road there is heartache too. That is part of life so it's how you cope with it, what you learn from it that's important. Don't lose those rose-coloured glasses of yours; that ability to believe in the good and always be using that lateral brain of yours to find the way to solutions and see them as challenges not problems. Always be kind, particularly to those who are lost in some way, and never stop looking for the way of belonging.

Maggie

MATT
TILLEY

Matt Tilley is a Melbourne-born radio presenter
and comedian, and is currently the co-host
of *Matt & Meshel – In the Morning* on KIIS
FM. In the highly competitive field of FM
breakfast radio in Melbourne, Matt's shows have
consistently reached number one more often
than any other over the past decade.

First, the bad news.

Your legs still rub together, your nostrils are still uneven and your arms are still so short they don't kink at the elbows when you put them in your pockets. But despite all those years of not wearing cords because of the noise they generated (banned from the library, how embarrassing!) and never being photographed with your head back in case people discovered your nasal asymmetry, you found that putting your hands in your pockets became one of the great joys in life – largely because it meant you were paying for somebody's treat and that usually put a smile on their face. So that was the great lesson – learning that making other people happy was a pretty good antidote for your insecurities. (Okay, so that kind of suggests money can buy happiness, but this is me writing this letter – not Jesus!) Because you have a short attention span I'm going to cram as much into some punchy thoughts as I can.

You're probably going to find out sooner or later that your real friends tell you the things you *need* to hear and the people who will fall away are the ones who tell you what you *want* to hear. And yes, it hurts. Because they are your friends and you want them to think everything about you is fantastic. But having relationships where people can be completely honest with you is what makes you stronger. And it also means that when they do say nice things, it REALLY means something.

No doubt people keep telling you that you shouldn't worry about what other people think. Be yourself. Be true to what you want to do. But in the end you'll realise that caring about what other people think can sometimes give you reason to stop and think. It probably makes you a bit more considerate of other people. And it probably gives you a bit of perspective. Particularly if there is a bit of a theme developing when it comes to all those external opinions. One person might be an idiot, two might be a coincidence, but three and it's probably you who are the problem. Four ... well, you should probably leave the country.

Okay, I can see your concentration waning and can hear your social media calling. I'll speed it up. And keep it random. People don't always love the person who's best at a sport – sometimes it's the hopeless one who tries the hardest or who is the biggest underdog (in hindsight, this makes you a sporting God!). The best laughs you will share will be about times when things go wrong. No one ever sits around laughing about the time things went perfectly. But nobody ever thinks this while things ARE going wrong. Try to. Regret of not having tried something lasts forever but pimples don't. No one ever likes kissing someone who's just had a cigarette. If you really want to do something, you will – even if you don't get the marks straight away. (You won't even get into your law course at first and then it will take 11 years ... and then you'll never use it.) Girlfriends (or boyfriends) don't make you a better or more complete person. Crying is not stupid. Different is not wrong. And finally, the funniest thing your parents can hear is, 'You don't understand – you have no idea what I'm going through!' They are SO annoying.

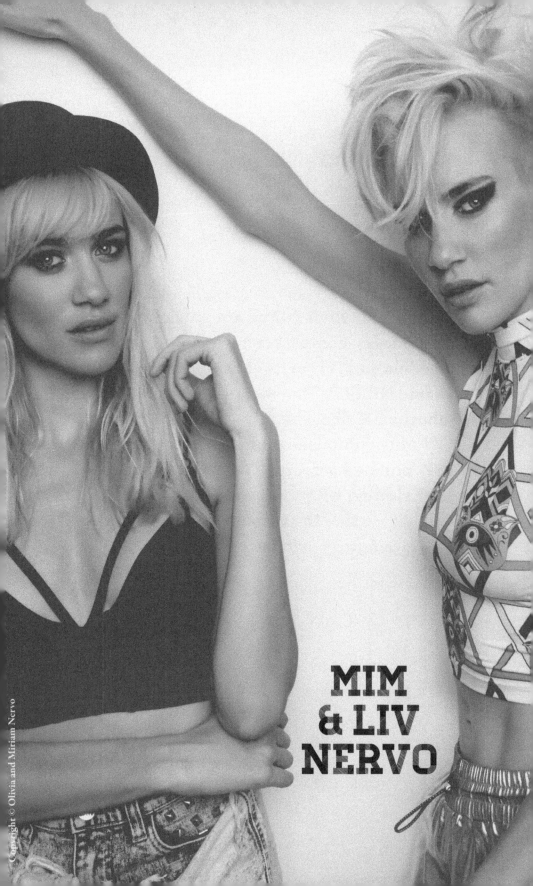

MIM
& LIV
NERVO

Miriam and Olivia Nervo are musicians, record producers, composers, singer–songwriters, models and DJs better known by their stage name NERVO. They were born and raised in suburban Melbourne. After signing with Sony/ATV Music Publishing at eighteen years of age, they pursued careers as songwriting partners. After signing with Razor Boy Music Publishing, they co-wrote the Grammy Award-winning single 'When Love Takes Over'.

Dear teenage Liv and Mim,

Your teens are a horrible age. It's okay to think this. We guarantee that 99.9% of the people in your classroom, school bus, choir etc. all think the same. Even if the popular kids look like they're having fun and they're 100% sure of themselves – they really aren't!

So, here is a brief survival kit.

1) Don't worry if the popular kids don't like you (they'll most likely end up fat, ugly and unhappy). It's hard to believe but, trust me – we've seen it happen! If you're at a school where you don't really like anyone then that's also okay. The world is a big place and you will find people (who are much cooler!) after school who you will connect with.

2) Don't waste your time worrying about what's cool or not. And there's no need to follow the crowd either. It's okay to be misunderstood, not 'normal' or just a bit weird. This just makes you more interesting in the future.

3) Do not get into any car if the driver has been drinking or doing any drugs – no matter how hot the boy may be. This is super important!

4) It's okay to experiment with alcohol and drugs but only very rarely and only around good friends. If you like it, then put it on hold for when you finish school. You'll be able to party a load when you're old enough to cope with a hangover and the responsibility to deal with what you're doing. Oh, and please also make sure while you are experimenting that someone in your group is sober in case you need to vomit (which you probably will).

5) As far as your career path goes, if you think there's something you want to do, or there's something you love doing or you're good

at, then please follow your passion. Reach for your dreams! Some dreams really do come true – we have seen it happen! Even if the career counsellor at school tells you that you can't be a pilot because you don't have perfect eyesight – just ignore them! In the future they'll have great new technologies like laser eye correction surgery which will make their point null. Anything is possible in the future and it's WAY too early to give up on your dream at your age, or ever! If you don't know what you want to do then that's also fine. Just make sure you keep an open mind and try finding a hobby. You will find your way.

6) We know Mum and Dad and your brother and sister annoy you but this is normal, and in the future you will understand them better and hopefully even be friends with them. We would recommend that you try to have patience in this awkward stage.

7) Remember we are our journey so all the turns you make will shape you. You are learning and will always keep learning. No one really has it figured out – they're all just pretending – so make sure you have a lot of fun along the way. Your happiness is your choice so CHOOSE to be upbeat, motivated and brilliant. Do not let others define you!

MISSY HIGGINS

Missy Higgins started singing when she was in her early teens, in Melbourne, and has become one of Australia's most popular artists since winning the triple j Unearthed competition in 2001. Her debut album *The Sound of White*, featuring the singles 'Scar' and 'The Special Two', won the ARIA Album of the Year and went platinum nine times.

Dear 13-year-old Me,

Look, I'm going to be honest: this year is going to be your toughest yet. You won't feel certain of anything. The world will sometimes feel like it is literally shifting underneath those brown leather T-bars of yours. That girl at school who you're afraid of: the one that everyone wants to be like, who pinches the back of your arm painfully every time you walk by? She is just a sad, sad person. I know it's hard to feel sympathy for her when you're currently fantasising about punching her in her stupid face, but at least try not to take it too personally and be glad you're not her.

Man, you don't know it now but there are soooooo many new hormones and stuff coursing through your veins that just make everything seem so emotional and raw, and HARD TO DEAL WITH. Believe me, when you get a bit older, life turns from a rickety old horror movie roller-coaster into a cruisy party sailing boat on a silken sea. OK, that's maybe an exaggeration but you get what I mean. Things will fall into place like a pro in a Tetris game. One by one. Stuff just begins to make sense.

Right now there are moments when it feels like you're never going to belong anywhere, right? That you're just too different? That no one could possibly understand a freaky alien like you? Well, just know this: some day in the not-too-distant future you'll realise that those qualities make you SO RAD. Seriously. Possibly even the exact things you're being teased for right now at school are the exact things that will gain you respect and many-a-high-five once you're out into the real world. Don't get me wrong, there are bozos everywhere who won't get you, even when you're 40 (and don't get me started on Twitter trolls) but unlike at school, when you're an adult it's easy to find people who get you and love you and accept you for who you are. And when you find those people, you've gotta pull them all real close and don't let them go. They are your friends for life. Bugger the rest!

Little friend, as the years go by your little guarded heart will unfold bit by bit, it will. You'll even learn to see the similarities between you and strangers, and realise we're not all so different after all. In fact you'll begin to see that most people are fundamentally the same, underneath all the many many layers of crap we build up over time to protect our papier-mâchéd hearts. You'll realise none of us has a friggin' clue what we're doing or how to live, we're just all doing the best we can. You'll be sad sometimes, I can't promise you that you won't because everyone gets sad. Some more than others. But you'll learn ways to deal with it (like exercising and not taking drugs ... also calling your sister and just talking and talking until the tightness dissipates) and importantly you'll notice that like everything, sadness comes and goes. Accepting the ride is often the hardest part. That and asking for help.

Honestly, darling, being a teenager sucks. I know it does. Being liked, being popular, being skinny, being pretty, getting good grades, pleasing your parents ... blurgh. Don't worry about those things. And please don't diet. Despite what ALL the magazines seem to be telling you, it's much better to be healthy than skinny. I know it feels like maybe the only thing that you can control in such a crazy, unpredictable world, but it is not the answer. Also, don't worry about your grades! If you really want to go to uni and get a degree, great. But if not, you should know that almost none of your friends who go to uni will end up using their degrees to get a job and *all* of them are still paying off their uni debts! If you know what you want to do, just get out there and find a way to do it! Be an apprentice, start from the ground up. Doing what you love is the most important thing in the world. But you've got a lifetime to figure out what that is. You've got a lifetime of learning, it never stops. And it's a cliché, I know, but life really does just get better and better. I promise. All you have to do right now is SURVIVE.

And know that I love you.

Love from older you.

xxxxxxx

NATASHA
STOTT
DESPOJA

Natasha Jessica Stott Despoja AM is Australia's Ambassador for Women and Girls. A former politician and former leader of the Australian Democrats, she was a Democrats senator for South Australia from 1995 to 2008. Stott Despoja hails from Adelaide and was appointed to the Senate at the age of twenty-six.

If you thought being Class Captain at the beginning of Year 8 was a one-off, you may need to reconsider.

It serves as a good introduction to leadership and duty; however, your teacher does insist on being greeted as 'Hail O Great One!', which provides a lesson in not always taking hierarchy too seriously.

Public service and public life will feature in your future, but be sure to maintain your sense of humour and always do your homework.

Your love of ballet, music and the arts will not wane. But you must cultivate it. Don't lose sight of the beauty and music in life. Perhaps schedule a little more time for cello practice.

Make time for the little things.

If you think life gets slower, it doesn't.

Your career options will not narrow as a result of your decade of ballet training coming to an end. You will go on to bigger and different things.

This is the year you cut your long hair. The shoulder-length blonde bob will serve you well for the years to come, but don't worry, in the next few years you will experiment with everything from short hair (even shaved a little) to different colours.

Keep your sense of style and try to have fun with clothes. Dressing up in a nice frock does not lower your IQ. It is about choice, no matter how women are portrayed. You'll see those superficial and double standards up close soon enough.

This is the year your history teacher will tell you off, albeit jokingly, for 'soiling' your text book with 'feminist' propaganda: you did put a women's liberation symbol on the cover of your history workbook.

Stay vigilant. If there is one thing we learn in the Women's Movement, it is that rights can be reversed and progress can slow.

Your role models include Senator Janine Haines and the author Germaine Greer. You will meet them both, and follow in the path of that pioneering Democrat Senator. She will launch your campaign to be a Senator in little over a decade.

That schoolgirl crush you have developed on that new boy in Year 8 won't go far. But you'll meet up at your school reunion in many years to come and laugh about it.

Know that you will have your heart broken at least once while you're still pretty young but real love will be intoxicating and special in a way that can't make sense right now.

You already understand, though – through your mum's life and work – that not all relationships are safe and sound. Gender equality and keeping women and children safe will be lifelong passions.

You know now how brave and feisty your feminist journalist mother, Shirley, is but you'll sharpen this perspective over the next few decades. Besides, you won't really cause her too much trouble in your teenage years, I promise!

Education is the key to so many things. It is the great equaliser.

Your mum has worked hard to get you a great education, but fees for tertiary education would break her. So watch out for the insidious debate about user-pays education.

That debate will grow, and you will become a key part of the fight for accessible and publicly funded education.

Your school motto *ex unitate vires* – 'in unity is strength' – is a belief that will guide you.

You will support those who are like-minded, even at some personal and professional cost.

Integrity is everything and you won't lose yours.

NATHAN
BUCKLEY

Nathan Buckley is a former professional
Australian rules football player, best known for
his time as captain of the Collingwood Football
Club in the AFL. He is currently the senior coach
of the Collingwood Football Club.

Nathan,

Knowing you well, I'm not sure if much of this will be absorbed!!

On the other hand, I know how sensitive you are to what people think of you, how influenced you can be by how they treat you and how the importance of 'being a good person' has become a big part of your make-up.

There are only two things I want to say to you today. The first is: you are special just as you are.

There will be moments of joy and sadness. You will feel pride and feel embarrassment. You will feel favoured at times and isolated in others. All of these emotions and events are to be embraced. They will teach you more about yourself and others. You will learn about your passions and your dreams through them.

One of the biggest influences on your happiness in the future will be to know yourself. To acknowledge the strengths you possess and to let them shine as often as you can. Don't be afraid of being less than perfect. It's OK.

The second is: be grateful for your life.

You have a loving family who care deeply for you. Your mum and dad have sacrificed much to provide you with the opportunity of a good education. You have a roof over your head and you never go hungry or want for the necessities in life.

The best way for you to remind yourself of these is one simple activity that will keep everything in perspective for you. Each night before you go to bed, write down three things that you are grateful for in your life. Keep looking for those things and you will always remember how blessed you are and, just as importantly, you will be in a great place to help others feel the same.

Live large, love freely and enjoy every moment.

Lots of love,

Your future self

NICK
LEE

Nick Lee is the Founder and CEO of The Jodi Lee Foundation, which he established soon after his wife Jodi lost her battle with bowel cancer in 2010. Leaving his role as a director of a multinational consumer goods company, Nick set out to help raise awareness of bowel cancer and educate people about the importance of screening for early detection.

Here is some advice to my teenage self ...

You never know what's coming around the corner. Your life can be changed in a heartbeat. Make the most of your opportunities. Live life to the fullest.

Don't sweat the small stuff and concern yourself with matters you can't control. There are so many things in life that are not worth worrying about. Too much stress can lead to health problems. Don't keep things bottled up – let them go.

Your happiness in life will largely be dictated by the relationships you have with your family, friends and colleagues. The best way to build and deepen your relationships is by making other people feel good. Ask yourself each day, 'What have I done to make someone feel good?' Try to be there for people when you are needed most.

Stand up for what you believe in. You will come across many doubters in your life. Don't let them get in the way of what you believe in and want to achieve. Have the courage to say 'no' if something doesn't feel right.

The more you put in the more you take out. Have a crack, jump in, don't procrastinate. You miss 100 per cent of the shots you don't take. Seek out new life experiences whenever you have the opportunity.

You will make mistakes – you're only human. Realise your mistakes, don't hide from them. Take responsibility and don't be afraid to say you are sorry. Your most important lessons come from making mistakes.

You can't control what happens to you but you can control how you react to it. If you get knocked down, get up! Try to make the best of every situation. Life will serve you many road bumps but just keep going.

Your integrity is so important. If you are honest, trustworthy and don't judge others, you will be happy with who you are. Don't be influenced by what other people think. Be your own person and people will respect you for it.

You don't know everything – ask questions, be curious and, above all, listen.

Take time to appreciate things and maintain childlike wonder. There are many beautiful things in this world – enjoy them. Don't let yourself get so bogged down in life that you miss out.

Your health is the most important thing. Invest in it so you can enjoy a long and healthy life. Follow your passions and believe in yourself. Work hard and love every minute of it. Look after yourself and the people you love, and laugh a lot.

PAUL
BANGAY

Paul Bangay is one of Australia's most renowned landscape designers. His beautiful and classically inspired gardens are celebrated around the world for their symmetry, rich detail and interesting palette. In 2001, Bangay was awarded the Centenary Medal for his contribution to public design projects, and has had his gardens displayed in many publications.

Dear 13-year-old Paul Bangay,

I am writing to you with all the experience and knowledge you have gained over the next 39 years. Your career in landscape design has served you well: it's facilitated much travel and financial security, allowed you to publish nine books and, most importantly, to indulge your passion. Passion has been key to your success; you can now, at the age of 13, already feel this passion as you potter around your parents' garden and experiment with neighbours' and friends' garden spaces. Follow this passion and do everything in your power to nurture it. This will involve travelling the world to explore gardens and new trends in landscaping, reading as many books and magazines as you can and, most importantly, experimenting. Experimentation is also key to success: don't be afraid to take risks and make mistakes. Even now, at my stage of life, I still make mistakes and am proud to own them. It's only through having the confidence to experiment that you will succeed. I now travel every year to look at gardens in all different parts of the world. I explore new countries as I try to find new sources of inspiration. I am never afraid to step out of my comfort zone in the pursuit of new experiences and adventures.

Confidence is key to selling your story; you will gain this by reassuringly creating more and more beautiful successful garden spaces. Every time you feel good about your result and every time a client appreciates what you have done you will gain more confidence. Everybody loves confidence: both in your personal and professional life it will be vital to your success.

Listen to people and what they have to say, and then work out how you can weave this into your way of thinking and expressing yourself. Clients in particular need to know you have their understanding but still want your talent and interpretation of their requirements. Be true to yourself. After listening to others' needs, don't proceed with a project or friendship if their values and style are at odds with your own. You may lose out on one job but you will win it back on another one where you will have far more integrity.

At your current age I know you have decided to make a career of your passion of garden design, but I also know you think it doesn't require a tertiary education to pursue this chosen career path. I am here now to tell you it does. My very wise father convinced me to attend Melbourne University to study a degree course in design, this is the best piece of advice anyone has ever given me and I was very wise to heed it. It's very important to have talent but without the technical education I would have never been able to succeed as I have. It's daunting at first but going to university was the best period of my life.

Paul, you have a distinct advantage in having a passion that you can make a career of. Follow this as far as you can, and I promise you this will serve you well.

Best of luck,

Your older self,

Paul Bangay

PETER
ALEXANDER

Peter Alexander is Australia's leading sleepwear designer. In 1987, he founded the brand Peter Alexander, selling designer lines of underwear and pyjamas, and it has since grown into an international company. Peter was awarded Australian Designer of the Year in 1992. He is a well-known supporter of animal rights and welfare.

I know school is hard, but your results at school, your so-called 'mark' is NOT as important in life as you think, or in any way your mark in life.

Who you are at school does not dictate who you are going to be after school. I know that remedial classes are embarrassing, I know having a stutter is hard and I know not being good at sport sucks. But again I want to say, I promise you that just because you're labelled a D student and don't fit in, this does not mean you're not going to be happy and successful in life.

I remember everyone around me was getting interested in the opposite sex, me not so much, I knew I liked boys but was so ashamed and confused. I am happy to tell you by the time you are just 10 years older, times will have changed and being gay, although still not a picnic while at school, is a lot more accepted and even celebrated. I know you get teased but so do most kids about all sorts of things. Kids will always find something to pick on as they need to help their own self-esteem; you just need one great friend.

Appreciate support at home to get through those school years. I promise you by 18 you are happy and have heaps of great friends. You will find your way, it just took a little longer than planned. While you are not on everyone's party list at school, trust me when I say your name becomes a loved household brand and you're invited to more things that you care to go to.

PETER DOHERTY

Peter Doherty was born in 1940 in Brisbane. After attending veterinary school at the University of Queensland and completing his PhD at the University of Ediburgh, he took up a post-doctoral position with the John Curtin School of Medicine Research. He made a breakthrough in discovering the role of T cells in the immune system, for which he received the Nobel Prize in Medicine and was named Australian of the Year.

The thought of writing to my 13-year-old self takes me back to 1953, the year I finished 8th grade in a Queensland state primary school and, a few months later, joined the first intake at Indooroopilly High School.

That meant catching the commuter steam train, then walking to this brand-new school on the hill. Back then, two things I would not have to tell that freckled, skinny kid would be 'Don't touch drugs' and 'Be careful of social media, it can waste your life!' Neither was on the horizon.

A regret is that I didn't talk more with the WWII refugee kids who were still flooding into Australia. The expectation was that they should become like us, not that we could learn from them. In fact, that's the main suggestion I'd make to my high school self today: interact with a much greater diversity of people and get a better understanding of different lives. Talking helps with your own choices. Life improves when we are less 'self' and more 'other' focused. With the really big issues like climate change, 'think globally, act locally'.

Raised by financially stretched parents ('frugals' who suffered the 1930s Depression) I didn't need a whole lot of advice about application and self-discipline. My imperative was to 'get the hell out of Dodge City', in this case a working-class outer suburb of Brisbane. Cheap paperbacks by (predominantly) European intellectuals and committed high-school teachers specialised in the sciences, arts and mathematics showed a way forward. That left me convinced that our socially diverse, immigrant country will only achieve its potential if all can access a quality education. That needn't include luxuries like overseas trips, but it does require great, well-paid and respected teachers.

If that 13-year-old were starting out today, I'd point to the advice I attribute to Dame Elisabeth Murdoch, who lived a full life to age 103: do everything the hard way, walk don't ride, take the stairs not the lift. Being happy is good, but we all experience unhappiness and, in fact, learn more from painful failure than from easy success. Just accept that as reality. Disneyland is fantasy, not life! Don't agonise, and forget any 'blame game'. That gets you nowhere.

At 13, we've got just about everything ahead of us. If I'd had better advice and more sophisticated parents, even older kids at high school to talk to, I would probably have done something quite different with my life, maybe in the area of writing or language. The consequence is, though, that I would not have won a Nobel Prize and I would now be a very different person. And, the absence of a senior group at school may (together with an early exposure to Protestant non-conformism) be why I've never had any problem in either ignoring peer pressure or in identifying authoritarians and bullies for who they are. Don't accept mindless conformism: do your own thing, look at the evidence and think for yourself. And when you get to that age, exercise your precious right to vote.

A couple of thoughts from Hamlet: 'Above all to thine own self be true' and 'We know what we are but know not what we may become'. Add to that: 'Showing up is half the battle.' Hang in there, learn as much as you can and seize opportunities when they're offered. Providing you make the effort and avoid doing major harm to yourself and to others, there's a good possibility that your experiences (both positive and negative) at age 13 and in the school years that follow will point to an interesting way forward. If that doesn't work, then any decent university offers a whole range of new and exciting options. Life is for the long haul. Delight in challenges, keep your mind open, and don't expect anything worthwhile to be easy!

Peter C Doherty,

University of Melbourne, 7 February 2016

PETER
GILMORE

Peter Gilmore, born and bred in Sydney, is the executive chef of Quay Restaurant in Sydney. Since 2001, Peter's creative and original cuisine has seen the restaurant receive an unprecedented number of Australian and international awards, and establish itself at the forefront of Australia's food scene.

Dear Peter,

I am writing to you as I know you have recently started high school.

School has always been a challenge on two fronts. One, having dyslexia has made it difficult, especially at this time when there is not a lot known about the condition. You puzzle your teachers, as you are able to comprehend concepts and express yourself verbally very well. When it comes to writing things down you are frustrated because you can't spell the words you want to write. As it turns out you will end up publishing two cookbooks with the aid of a thing called 'spell check' and a wife who happens to be very good at writing and patient enough to be your scribe.

On the second count you have always been a bit chubby. It's hard fighting genetics. You will conquer it in your twenties but by your forties you will find yourself still fighting the battle. As a young child this made you a target at school, and it wasn't just the bullies. Kids can discriminate easily. Without life experience their reactions can be very superficial and quite hurtful. In a lot of ways these experiences, though hurtful, have made you quite resilient and through this a strong belief in yourself has prevailed.

What it has taught you is a deep empathy for people's differences and a certain level of humility that will keep you grounded. In future the sort of success you will have professionally may have made you arrogant but some of the challenging experiences you have had at this age will help you keep things in perspective and will allow you to remain humble and appreciative.

I feel that creativity needs to come from a place of quiet confidence and humility, as it is a 'gift'. You will feel very lucky that you are able to express yourself creatively through your work.

I would also like to tell you that the only friends worth having at high school are the ones that accept you for who you are. I know you have recently moved house and have started at a high school where you know no one. As it turns out, you are not the only one in that situation and you soon make a couple of good friends.

Friendship is about give and take, and it is worth finding people who are genuine. This is something you will always seek.

To finish, I want you to know that although life is full of ups and downs and challenges, I have found that remaining positive and truly believing in yourself is the best way forward. Find your passion and live that passion to the best of your ability.

You will enjoy yourself along the way,

Peter

RACHAEL
MAZA

Rachael Maza is an Australian actress, narrator and director. She has acted in the film *Radiance* and on stage in *The Sapphires*, and worked as a TV presenter on ABC's *Message Stick* and SBS's *ICAM*. She is currently working as part of The Black Arm Band. In 2007, she and her sister began co-writing an autobiographically inspired theatre show *Sisters of Gelam*.

Hi Rachael,

I know this will sound really odd, but I'm writing to you because I am actually you, but a lot older – in fact I'm now 50 ... I can hardly remember being you. 13? I know I was in year 8 in Dover Heights High School, an all-girls school in the eastern suburbs of Sydney whose claim to fame was that Ita Buttrose and Renée Geyer went there. I remember my best friends: Renee, the Jewish redhead with braces, and Naomi, who lived in the same street – Stafford St Paddington – and was your handball/tomboy buddy. And her house was always riddled with mangy cats! I know you quite enjoy school. You're actually quite good at most subjects including Maths, Science and Music.

Although you have a couple of good friends, you're really quite shy ... You won't always be shy! And if it's any consolation, those bloody big buck front teeth of yours (one with the big white mark) won't always be the bane of your existence – in fact, even though you never get braces they sort of sort themselves out. Also you finally get the white one capped and eventually you never even think about your teeth at all ... in fact, you even get compliments about how good your teeth are. How funny is that!

I laugh when I think about that time some girls threatened to bash you up – inviting you to meet them at the basketball court after school – but they didn't show. I admire that about you: you really were strong in your principles, and always quick to defend others who were being treated unfairly. This didn't go unnoticed. Many years later a woman came up to me. She introduced herself to me saying we went to school together. I looked hard and thought maybe I recognised her, but really

I didn't. She said, 'I remember you because you were one of the only ones who talked to me even though I was fat.' So I guess your sense of fairness and equality made some people's lives along the way a little easier.

One thing I would like to say to you, though, is, 'I know you think of yourself as indistinct, even invisible, but trust me – you're not!' I look back at photos of you and you're such a beautiful young woman, maybe a little gangly, but with a beautiful smile and heart, and I wish you could know that now, back then ... I wish you could enjoy your beauty, your warmth, your generosity, your humanity, and know how you inspire this in others. In fact I wish you could sit with me now and look back at all these photos and laugh with me ... and see the absurdity of it all. I could tell you of all the wonderful adventures you will have, how you will have little tastes of love, little tastes of a career, but actually you will always be the same you that even 40 years later is not looking for the end goal, not aiming for this thing called success.

In fact you will continue to take life as it comes, each adventure as it unfolds, always open to what comes next, never staying in any one thing for too long ... (That's not entirely true – this last job has lasted over seven years, which, let me tell you, is a world record!) But you will mostly always be happy!

One thing to note, though – the secret to your happiness is keeping healthy and being in and amongst people. Your hardest times will be when you let your health go down and lose touch with the people who matter to you. But I guess you can only learn this for yourself and maybe even that was a valuable lesson you will need to have.

Anyway, have a great life, I know you will. The biggest thing for you to remember is to love the you that you are at any given moment.

This will take you a long time to learn, but maybe you can get there a little quicker than I did ... Because at the end of the day – it's all codswallop anyway – life is what you are living right now and nothing else, so enjoy it now!

Also, I just want you to know how much I love you.

Big hugs,

Rachael

RAFAEL
EPSTEIN

Rafael Epstein is a journalist who has worked in Sydney, Melbourne, Canberra, Timor, Indonesia, Europe and the Middle East. He has also worked at the Investigative Unit at the *Age*. Rafael currently hosts the *Drive* program on 774 ABC Melbourne. His first book, *Prisoner X*, was published in March 2014.

Dear teenage Raf,

What you should know is that you will grow up into a magnificent young man. That's the good news. The bad news is it doesn't happen overnight. It will take a long time, longer than you have been on this little planet. It doesn't happen easily because becoming a man is not some natural process that you intuitively grow into.

Have you noticed that you are not growing into your body right now? That so many of the other teenagers around you are bigger and have bodies that look like they will grow into a man? Well that will happen to you, even though the pace seems, right now, like it is more than glacial. The bad news is that growing into becoming a man is even tougher. In fact it is the hardest thing that you will do.

You will find someone who loves you just as fiercely, even more spectacularly than the heat you feel inside you right now, for some of the girls that float in and out of your life. And in fact you already have most of what you need to find a job and an identity in the outside world. Your profession is waiting for you. It will fit you like a man's hand fits perfectly inside a beautifully tailored leather glove. You know how you don't know what you want to be when you grow up? Don't worry. Actually, you do know what you want to be. It will come with much hard work and some searching and some dithering along the way. But it is far from your toughest task.

What will come close to breaking you, what will threaten to tear you to pieces, what will give you the greatest succour and joy, even as it gives you the most anxious moments of your life, will be the very making of you. Becoming a man is about finding out who you really are.

How you live, how you connect, how you rise to anger, how you give up your own needs, wants and desires for those you truly love. How you learn to foster your character, channel your passions, carve out your identity and enjoy the essence of being you; that is what it means to become a man.

How you think of sex, what you do when you dream of it, how you physically respond to a lover's demands, to be sure these are a core aspect of what it means to be a man. They can be a foundation but they are nowhere near a complete picture of what it means to tell the difference between desire and true engagement, between loving and taking. It takes time to feel your way into the visceral difference between strength and anger, between providing the solid soil that can allow true love to grow, and simply being strong like the rock that love merely flows over. This is the toughest part of your life. You will need to take a close look at the fibres of your soul, and the toughest reaches of your emotions. But this is the most rewarding part of being alive. So remember to breathe and revel in your hedonism, for they are the simplest of pleasures, but you will even more greatly relish that which you work so hard to understand.

RICHARD
JOSEPH
FRANKLAND

Richard Joseph Frankland is a playwright, scriptwriter and musician. He is an Aboriginal Australian of Gunditjmara origin from Victoria. He has worked as a soldier and a fisherman, and as a field officer to the Royal Commission into Aboriginal Deaths in Custody.

Dear Richard,

Hey, it's me, or you and me. You're a teenager and I'm 51 now.

I've seen war, investigated deaths in custody, had typhoid, had bands, been a soldier, buried more family than I care to mention, fallen in love, out of love, laughed, danced, fallen over, got back up, cried big tears and sobbed hard. I've been a hero and I've failed. I've saved lives and changed lives. I've written books, albums, plays, films, poems some for the public and some secret ones.

I've had children.

They are beautiful. So beautiful that sometimes I cry just thinking of them.

What should I tell you?

Your brother Shane, you'll never stop missing him. Same with your sister Linda, you'll never stop missing both of them. You'll never get over the grief. But it's OK, 'cause later on you'll learn that grief is love.

You'll get your heart broken, a few times, and it will hurt. But you'll learn from it, and believe me you learn to love again.

Our dad said to have a good sense of right and wrong, and even though he died when we were six, we must have remembered it from somewhere. Maybe when he was holding us when we were young. You're going to help a lot of people. Some you'll never know that you've helped. It will happen with your films, your speeches, your actions.

One day you'll learn that it's okay to be involved in so many people's lives. To have so many people depend on you. Just remember, when life slaps you down, get up and slap the bastard back. Hard. Never give up. But know when to be graceful in defeat.

I love this poem: you'll write it when you're dead broke, and feeling lonely, and it will make you strong.

Singing to the World
Richard J Frankland

If I were to look back at this life of mine
At times of folly, foolishness
At times of joy and conquest
At times of sadness, times of repenting
Times of great victories and times of smaller ones
Both of equal importance and equal meaning
At times when the world had crashed and the scars on my soul
Were unequalled in pain and sorrow
I would smile at my silliness
Be embarrassed at my joy, my ego, my loves and losses
Celebrate my victories and my times of losing
rejoice in my recognition of the equality of a smile and the meaning of a gift and
the beauty of a soul
I would shed tears at my times of sadness
And chase bittersweet memories across the dreamscape of the memories of my life
And finally I would lay exhausted with my heart laying rent open upon the
hearth of my home
And I would sift through it searching for diamond drops of memories

And if one would see me in such a state
they would be prone to ask, 'What would you change?'
Nothing, not one thing, I would say
Then, after a contemplative moment
Except I would say whilst challenging myself
Whilst drawing a sword of courage and casting aside a shield of shame
I would shout loudly to the world
I would have sung louder,

Smiled brighter
given harder
seen beauty quicker
shared smiles more often
hugged harder
loved better
I would learn to play my soul better
I would paint teardrops so I could find happiness easier
I would have danced with more abandon and with more people
And also rejoiced in dancing alone
I would laugh at the small problems so I could help solve the big ones
I would
see dreams in clouds and taste the future in morning dew
I would find thoughts profound in flames
And see the wondrous beauty in a small rock, a leaf, a single blade of grass in a
piece of bark upon a tree.
From this I would know what makes a view majestic and a soul so
small yet so big
I would worship the spirits of the untainted ones, the children, the meek, those
unable to protect themselves
I would strive to heal the evils of the world and learn to love with an open hand
I would learn to write songs of humility and to plant seeds of hope and healing
Then I would turn to the one who asked the question and say
What about you? What will you change?
What should I tell you?

Dance, love, sing, be balanced, fall over, get back up, make the world a better place, play music, write, act, build, fall in love. With everyone, but mostly fall in love with yourself.

Best,

Richard

SHARON
LEWIN

Sharon Lewin is a professor, infectious diseases physician and scientist, and is internationally renowned for her research into all aspects of HIV disease and pathogenesis. She is the director of The Peter Doherty Institute for Infection and Immunity, a joint venture of the University of Melbourne and Royal Melbourne Hospital, and was named Melburnian of the Year in 2014 for her achievements in her field.

To my teenage self,

No matter how you are feeling right now – overwhelmed with school, fitting in with friends and being understood by family – exciting and unexpected opportunities and challenges but also great things lie ahead for everyone. Never forget that.

When I was your age and living in suburban Melbourne in 1975, I felt trapped in a boring place which seemed far, far away from where things were really happening. Who could have imagined how the world would change in the next 30 years? Melbourne is now a city with its own distinctive style. Melbourne now leads in design, research, sport, food and fashion, and at the same time embraces diversity and inclusion in all it does. It's a city I greatly enjoy and am now immensely proud to live in. At the same time, through advances in technology, the world has also now come to us. So your world now is likely to be a very different world in the future, one you might have never imagined.

A few words of advice for managing the changing world ahead ...

The great adventures and successes in life come to people who are open to others, open to change and open to hard work. So embrace the opportunities that come to you and always say 'yes' whenever you can. 'Yes' should be the default position.

Be kind – to everyone. When I was five, my mum insisted I always say 'yes' to every party invitation – no matter who it was or whether I would know anyone there. From as early as I can remember, this was the rule. Be kind to everyone you meet in life or in work. Other people's stories are always inspiring.

At times, life can seem overwhelming. It's hard to know how to manage your time to juggle study (and later work) and play effectively but it's important to get right. At times, it seems easier to just shut yourself off from the rest of the world when you are under pressure and just focus on one thing. But life is never like that. We are always part of a larger community and world. This difficult juggle will continue forever so learning a balance that works is important. None of us get it right all the time.

Enjoy the journey in life – not just the destination. At different times in life, priorities will change. This may seem a distraction but don't resent this. You may need to alter the balance of life along the way but that's part of the journey to enjoy.

Follow your passion. People excel in their careers and in life when they are doing what they love or what they care about. I know not everyone is lucky enough to find that but if you can, and can make money too, treasure that. A successful career in medicine and science, for me, often required extremely hard work, long hours and some sacrifice. This is much easier to do if you are passionate about what you do.

Family and friends always come first. Never miss a major life event for a friend or family member. Doesn't matter where or when or how inconvenient, make every effort to be there.

Travel as much as you can. Travel is even better with a safe and enriching home base. Travel introduces you to new aesthetics, new ways of looking at the world and most importantly, new people. It is also a reminder that despite all our differences there is a common humanity in the world. Regardless of where you live, your colour, your religion, all human life is equal and everyone deserves respect. Growing up in a rich country means we have an opportunity, perhaps a responsibility, to give back and try to eliminate that inequality.

Make sure you live somewhere different from where you grew up – anywhere will be wonderful but spending time in a place at the epicentre of whatever you are interested in can be transformative. For me, in HIV medicine in the late 90s, that was the Rockefeller University in New York. This was the beginning of life-saving treatments for people living with HIV and New York was where much of this research was happening. Moving to New York with my husband and two young children seemed a tremendous hassle at the time but the benefits personally, professionally and as a family stay with us all forever.

As a woman, there will always be extra pressures on you. I doubt this will ever change. Even with the great advances in equality for women, which I have enjoyed in my own career, there are still many additional challenges for women. See these as extra advantages and opportunities, not drawbacks. Having a family and perhaps remaining the primary caregiver is a great privilege with immense rewards; being able to combine that with a career too is an even greater joy.

And finally, as Mary Schmich, a journalist for the *Chicago Tribune* (and not Kurt Vonnegut), famously once wrote for a hypothetical commencement speech (which you should read), wear sunscreen! The scientists were right – it works! It will keep you looking young. If only we had been told that in the 70s!

SHAUN
TAN

Shaun Tan is an artist, writer and filmmaker. He won an Academy Award for *The Lost Thing*, a 2011 animated film adaptation of a picture book he wrote and illustrated in 2000, and he has published many other acclaimed books such as *The Red Tree* and *The Arrival*. He was born in Fremantle, Western Australia, in 1974 and grew up in the northern suburbs of Perth.

What should I say to you, my thirteen-year-old self?

Well, I can't believe how young you look in that picture, not really thirteen, more like a little kid. Actually, I do recall that this was a slight problem at the time, compounded by being unusually short. (I still am, sorry to say, nothing much changes! Your hair is a lot thinner, that's about it.) I know that your appearance makes you particularly self-conscious at a time when self-consciousness is probably your defining neurosis – you are even self-conscious about being self-conscious, and self-conscious about that too, and so on. Being half-Chinese in suburban WA in the 1980s, a place and time when it is rather uncool to be Asian in any way, offers no great advantage. But hey, believe it or not, being mixed race is a good thing here in the twenty-first century. Multiculturalism has come a long way, in spite of setbacks. As a writer and illustrator (which is what you end up doing – as an actual job, crazy huh?) you will get asked all the time about your cultural identity, in a *positive* light. Yeah, I know, try telling that to teenagers throwing beer cans and slurs at you from a passing car on your way to school! Never mind those idiots, they only want you to acknowledge their idiocy. Times change and society moves on, so that's one bit of good news. The future is just another word for hope. Being a nerd actually turns out to be a good thing too – you end up winning an Oscar for it. I know, it's nuts.

But yes, there is quite a chasm between then and now. Can you believe that I/you/we are old enough now to have been thirteen three times over? Yikes. I realise I could have learned quite a few other languages in that time, as proficiently as English, but I'm still boringly monolingual. So try and learn another language maybe. Chinese would be handy. Actually now that I think about it, you *are* learning Chinese at thirteen, but you can't see the point and will stop in a couple of years to study other things. Note to present-day self: still time to learn Chinese.

On the other hand, you just never know what you are going to need. My wife is Finnish (spoiler alert!) so now I'm learning Finnish, alongside my two-year-old daughter (spoiler alert!). Alas, Finnish is not exactly on the curriculum at Balcatta High in Western Australia circa 1987. This could have been *erittäin kätevä* (very handy). Instead you are going to spend long hours studying physics and higher mathematics in senior high school, only to find that you can't even do long division at forty, and that you were never really suited to engineering. As an artist (final spoiler I promise) you just don't need to know that much about sinewaves, algebra or how much a bowling ball weighs in a descending lift. Actually that's not true: I've referred to maths and physics quite a bit when writing at least one book, so who knows about these things. Education of any kind is rarely a waste of time. All I can suggest is, 'the broader the better'. Take an interest in *everything*. You never know what you will need later on.

The future, like hope, is unpredictable. Any advice from older to younger versions of one's self – and by extension to any other younger person, which is the real purpose of this letter I imagine – is a tricky business. I can't advise you, the thirteen-year-old, much on content without disrupting the whole experience or else appearing mightily out of touch (we live in very different worlds now, as do current thirteen-year-olds). You just have to find out for yourself. You might as well be giving advice to me! There are certain wisdoms as a teenager that may

From *Tales from Outer Suburbia*,
Allen & Unwin, 2008

well be forgotten as an older person, as insightful as anything else. You may know this from talking with your parents. Why can't they grasp basic concepts? Didn't they used to be thirteen too?

A few years ago I wrote a story about a very wise water buffalo living in a vacant lot, which local people would frequently consult when they had a problem. The water buffalo was unable to speak and too lazy to move, so would just point in a particular direction: nobody had any idea what this meant, only that they had the option of investigating further, by themselves, to see what the buffalo might be pointing at. I think the best advice is just like that: the most anyone can do is point vaguely. You can't actually tell anyone much in advance and expect it to have the same weight of personal experience. That's hot, so don't touch it. Better yet, touch it so you know what I mean by 'hot'. My advice about hotness is now moot. So maybe I should say nothing at all, let things go as they will, rather than risk screwing everything up as happens in a time-travel movie. Enjoy being thirteen!

What's that? Well, yes, there is one problem. Being thirteen is not really a lot of fun. At least not for me, and I'll bet not for a lot of other people. That's not to say it's not also a happy time, full of wonderful experiences, insights and opportunities. It just seems very difficult and awkward, and not even in hindsight. Thirteen-year-olds know the awkwardness acutely, each and every day. You can't ignore it. It's waiting for you first thing every morning.

Aside from the usual problems of a transitional phase, a messy crossing from childhood to adulthood, you probably don't have a great deal of autonomy, cash-flow or career satisfaction, to say the least. Decisions are still often made for you and punishments dished out, and school may start feeling grimly institutional, as if you are doing time.

'What are you in for?'

'Being thirteen, but if I behave myself I might be eligible for parole in a few years.'

'Just watch out for those thugs in the exercise yard, and don't upset the warden.'

I exaggerate, but you know well what I mean.

Social relationships are tricky, if not sometimes mortifying, especially in relation to the opposite sex. Parents don't have a clue about what's going on. Adults are patronising. Previously respected authority figures are turning out to be very flawed human beings. The rules of society seem increasingly arbitrary, not to mention grossly unfair, not to mention insane (you know because you watch the news). You suspect that some classmates are actually undiagnosed psychopaths. There are mood swings too, as if you need that on top of everything else. You probably don't know where you are going, what you are going to be, or who you are right now, or where you fit in the world at all. When people ask, you have a tendency to shrug, and you long to be left alone to ruminate on all this in a cave of your choice.

My older self can offer good news and bad news on this front. Which do you want first? Okay, the bad news is that such social and identity anxieties are unlikely to disappear. The world is still kind of messed up. Confidence and satisfaction levels will always be problematic if you are any kind of thinking or sensitive person (which I hope I am, it's a good thing to be). You will often wonder, for the rest of your life, where you fit in, what you are supposed to be doing, who you are and so on. That uncertainty comes and goes all the time, there's a fair amount of depression too. Learn to live with it!

So what's the good news? All this is no bad thing. There's nothing wrong with having some degree of insecurity, and it means that you probably *are* a thinking and sensitive person. And while it can feel like an affliction, you can also learn ways of managing it, improve things, and you might even find it useful. Anxiety is an important part of being alive and awake in the world. Of course, if it gets too much, you don't have to tough it out alone in your bunker: there are always people who care about you and can help. It should never be allowed to get extreme, but on the other hand, I don't think it should disappear entirely. I imagine that at eighty, if I make it that far, I'll probably still be worrying over questions of identity, purpose and meaning from my hovering scooter. I kind of hope so. I think it goes hand in hand with creativity and curiosity. I can't write or paint without some strange mix of confidence and insecurity; it's as if one can't exist without the other.

So, if the water buffalo could talk, it would probably just say this: it's okay to be worried. It's okay to be afraid, depressed, even miserable at times. And then it would point off into the distance: just keep going anyway. It might help to know that you are hardly alone, hardly abnormal. Everyone around you is dogged by anxiety and doubt, and most of us are going to great lengths to conceal it. Especially those who make themselves out to be super self-assured and confident – there's all sorts of crazy things going on under the cool tip of the iceberg. Actually, be a little wary of those ones.

I wouldn't worry about your future too much either – let your other selves, like me, do that for you. There will be plenty of pressure on you in a few years, if not now, to make career decisions. Yes, by all means pick a direction, fill in forms and keep an eye on grades, but do keep in mind that you are likely to have multiple careers in your lifetime. In hindsight, I think the main purpose of school is not academic achievement (as you are thinking now) or attaching numbers to a sheet. Scores are not very important in the scheme of life. Study hard, but don't do it for a bunch of stupid percentages. School should be about finding your passion.

In choosing a career, or having life choose one for you, I doubt that anything is more important than passion. Forget about income, status or family respect – those things follow from doing good work and diligent study, and good work and diligent study follow from passion, which is a very personal, non-exchangeable resource. Yours is the only kind there is. Imagine that in the future your job is actually a fun, fulfilling hobby for which you get paid. This is certainly possible: I'm doing it right now. Whatever you are enjoying the most at thirteen, you will likely still enjoy at twenty, forty, eighty. The passion will grow, wane, develop, even radically change course, but at its core, the thirteen-year-old self is an excellent time to know what inspires and motivates you the most, prior to the various complications and compromises of adulthood. In fact, when things get really tough and confusing as hell, you are going to need motivation, and it won't come so much from strategy or knowledge: it will come from passion. Things you find inspiring and fun. I don't think they talk about fun enough in relation to careers, but it's a pretty vital component.

As a forty-one-year-old, I don't feel that my basic interests have changed much at all since I was thirteen, and I'm glad I pursued painting and drawing, in spite of so many people telling me that being an artist did not constitute stable employment.

Interestingly, the kind of job I do now did not exist on the charts presented by my career counsellor in high school: a terrific guy, but like the rest of us unable to know everything, much less the future. In any case, he was better off remaining vague, because the path by which I came to be, say, directing a short animated film, writing a picture book, painting a mural or speaking at a conference in Mexico is so crazily convoluted, I could not have actually studied for it directly. And I didn't: nothing I do now is the consequence of actual qualification, I've just learned along the way, moving from project to project, with lots of flat spots in between. I may well be doing something quite different in another ten years, and I'm open to that. The most important thing I learned at school – which you are learning now – is how to adapt, learning how to learn. The algebra you will forget, but the experience of wrangling formulae, even the insufferably boring stuff, is lodging an important pattern somewhere in your subconscious, building some kind of wiring and stamina.

And get used to all that studying, my friend, because you never stop being a student. The idea of high school or any other graduation is just a passing formality. It doesn't end! You never really graduate, you just move on to the next area of study. The exams do end, though, which is terrific.

Okay, so this is my advice in a nutshell: just follow your passion. Be interested in whatever seems to keep you interested. Not especially original or profound advice. And yes, I know you already know this. But the thing is, at this point in your life, you are also sensing a lot of things getting in the way, mainly that anxiety I already mentioned. Just try not to worry so much. Career-wise, things go up and down but seem to pan out nicely enough, so far at least! I wouldn't mind some tips from my eighty-year-old self, come to think of it. But I guess he'd probably just say the same stuff.

As for other non-career matters, all the personal thirteen-year-old hang-ups which I won't even get into here – some things are best kept personal – well, it all works out fine. Not perfectly, because there is no such thing. The main problem, in hindsight, is really just anxiety itself. Everything seems so big and consequential. And it is, but so are you. If more people knew that at a young age, we could spend a lot more time just being ourselves and doing what we do best.

I think that's about it. Good luck!

Oh, just one more thing. Many years from now, you will be travelling in Paris and you will come across a large table of different cheeses at a social function. Do not eat this cheese! No good will come of it. Even if you ignore everything else I've just said, trust me on this one.

Simon Reeve is a television presenter and host for the Seven Network. He is currently sport presenter on *Weekend Sunrise* and was the host of *Million Dollar Minute* and *It's Academic.* He was born in Perth and is the son of former news presenter Earl Reeve.

Dear Simon,

Firstly those pimples will go away, eventually. Purple flares may also come back into fashion ... after the next Bronze Age. The cool kids may seem cooler, untouchable right now, but hang in there, fella. The dags may not inherit the earth, but the distribution system will be more equitable.

One day, believe me, you will appreciate how much a secure, safe home environment and a household full of people who love and care about you will become the foundation stone for your life. It will be the framework around which you see the world. For sure you will stumble and fall along the way, making mistakes, sometimes letting people down. Just know there is a strong, unshakeable moral code in place to help teach you right from wrong.

Be wary of the vanity of your physical self. There will be days when you think you are king of the world. You ain't. Encourage that guy to put down the gel and the hair dryer (while you have hair), walk away from the mirror and go read a book.

Compassion, humility, tolerance, respect. These are the ancient creeds to live by. On the flip side, jealousy, malice, revenge and hatred are terribly destructive forces in this world. Drive around them, sidestep them and silence them whenever you feel they're gathering to find a voice inside you. Ignorance is never an excuse for an error of judgement.

A healthy and positive attitude, a ready smile, will take you places. From the cleaner at work to the boss, from the poor to the rich, treat everyone the same. They are all forging a living, supporting families; doing their best. Let dignity and integrity become your calling cards.

Keep an open heart, an open mind and an open door. People the world over are much more the same than they are different. Let art and music move you to tears. Forever embrace nature and animals. Let the dog up on the couch. Step outside into the rainstorm. Marvel at the sunset and the first frangipani flower in spring. Hitch your heart and soul to the beauty of the world around you.

Many (but not all) of the bumper stickers for life glow with the light of emotional truth. Great lessons come from adversity. Trust your instincts. Don't be a victim. Never take things for granted. Don't fear or run from loneliness. Real mean do cry. Little things mean a lot. Appreciate where you came from.

Often overwhelming fear of failure and harrowing anxiety knock in the depth of night or hijack you when you least expect. It's part of who you are. It may take a very long time to reach a negotiation, but one day you will understand. Call it the way of things.

And finally, whatever happens, find your way to Africa. To hear the call of a lion across a still night in the Okavango, to smell wild sage for the first time, will touch something deep within. I can't easily explain, but you will know what it is and it will change you.

Don't realise too late that it's not about you. Your own children will teach you more about yourself than you will ever know.

Now get back outside and I'll yell out when dinner's ready.

SOPHIE
LEE

Sophie Lee is a film, stage and television actress and author from Newcastle, New South Wales. She starred in the 1994 film *Muriel's Wedding* and earned a nomination for the Australian Film Institute Award for Best Supporting Actress for her role in the 1997 film *The Castle*.

Dear Soph,

Take a seat close to the front and mentally focus on these two words. Put them up in pastel bubble writing if you like: Dream Big. You can't always control the way things pan out but you will *always* be surprised by what you can accomplish when you aim high.

So keep dreaming, the bigger the better. Now please tuck those name-tags into your socks, there's a girl making her way down the aisle of this bus who is looking for ammunition to make your life hell and hand-sewn labels on school socks will seem like a good start to someone like her.

These school bus rides through the outer suburbs of Newcastle won't go on forever – although some days they'll feel like it. Bus rides from hell come and go but real friends are forever – isn't that the way the expression goes? Ignore her and stay strong. Mentally stick your fingers in your ears. This too will pass.

Weren't you excited over breakfast 30 minutes ago? You're going to meet some amazing like-minded people at your new school. One girl in particular will get you when you're being 'you'. She'll understand your quirky sense of humour *and* share your passion for poetry, drama, the complete works of David Bowie, amateur photography and the taste of homemade bread. She's waiting to meet you at your new Senior School where sooner than you know it you'll be swapping Jumping Jacks and hilarious anecdotes.

Forgive your mum for sewing your name-tags into your socks.

Hey, I recognise that cold, tight feeling in the top of your chest. I still get it myself sometimes. The feeling when you sense you're on the wrong side of a sheet of glass. Believe me, soon the stars will align, things will turn your way and you'll be on the reverse side – the popular side. But it's precisely at that time that you should remember to be kind. There's always going to be someone on the wrong side of the glass, so make them feel included, doesn't matter how small the gesture. Being cool is never more important than being kind.

Oh, and by the way? Stop worrying. You worry too much. Chances are you're probably not going to be bitten by a funnel web, develop a rare childhood cancer or fall off a cliff this afternoon, but you will make yourself feel sick if you stew on things that are beyond your control. Being heckled on the school bus will probably be easier to endure if you tell someone about it. Sometimes help is closer than you think. A single worry can turn into an army of bull ants if you don't shut it down fast, and you can do just that by talking to a school counsellor, a parent, a sibling or a friend.

I wish you had worked harder on your embouchure. Do more music practice!

Oh, speaking of mouthpieces. Be brave! Join the school wind ensemble. You love to write – offer to edit the school magazine. You enjoy public speaking? Explore both debating team and drama society. So... you're not great at sport? Just because you'll never be the fastest doesn't mean it's not good for you to be part of a team. Get in there. You'll always feel better once you've exercised.

Push the bell. This bus ride is nearly over and I can see the school gates at the bottom of the hill. Ignore those backseat bullies, they'll move on to torturing insects once they see they can't crack this little nut. Keep busy. Head high. Goodbye Gina Troutface, don't let the bus door hit you on the way out.

Remember to be kind. Dream big. Hell, let your name-tags hang right out of your socks. Today is the first day of the rest of your life.

Soph

STEPHANIE RICE

Stephanie Rice is a retired competitive swimmer who hails from Brisbane. She won three gold medals at the 2008 Summer Olympics in Beijing. She was awarded the Medal of the Order of Australia on 26 January 2009. Stephanie was also the 2008 Telstra Swimmer of the Year, and the 2008 World Swimmer of the Year.

Dear Steph,

What an exciting journey you are on!!! There are so many things about to unfold for you so keep your thoughts positive. I know at times it feels like you aren't understood and you feel alone, but don't worry as you will work through all of those fears and find some incredible friends who will last you through life.

Your love for swimming will continue to grow and the path that lies ahead for you is one that will blow your mind with excitement, joy and fulfilment. You never could have predicted or even dreamed of the success you will have. But don't worry about results and outcomes, as all of that is just a by-product of the love and passion you have for the water.

There will be challenges and hard times, like on any journey to the top, but trust me when I say that all the tears and nights where you lay in bed worried and doubtful, that they will all be worth it. Those moments are a test of character and you must always remember that they are happening for a reason ... everything happens for a reason.

You are about to embark on some big changes. You will find a coach who will mentor and lead you towards incredible things, not only in the pool but also through life. This man is an angel on earth and you will forever be grateful for the love and light he continually shares with you and the wisdom and guidance he provides. He understands you better than anyone else and you will form a very strong bond together. He will always be there to pick you up when you're down and be there to celebrate in the successes. Without him you know that you wouldn't be the woman that you will become.

Be grateful and thankful for the supporting and loving family that you have. I know at times it is challenging and you will always long for freedom and independence, but know that your parents love you dearly and truly do want the best for you. They love you as Stephanie Rice, not Stephanie Rice the Swimmer, and over time you will truly appreciate that deep love.

Your family will always come together to support you and be there at every meet to watch you put all your hard work to the test! They will be the ones you look for in the stands as you step out of the pool after victories, but also the ones who will hold you and comfort you after the struggles.

Swimming is a huge part of your life and always will be, but there will always be more to life than swimming. You are continually guided towards your path and trust that every decision you make is the right one, even though if at the time it feels otherwise. Know inside that there are lessons and blessings in each decision and turning point, and you will always have the support system to help you through when you are unable to do it on your own.

One day you will look back and be able to write a letter similar to this that will help others towards their journey to success. Writing this letter will not only inspire other young athletes, but the process of writing this will also heal elements within yourself.

When times get tough, always remember to ask for help and take time to turn inwards and reflect. Don't be too hard on yourself, as I know you can be at times, rather use this energy to empower yourself and others.

You will always be most fulfilled when you give back to and share your insights and experiences to empower others, so know that this journey you are on is to gather the knowledge so one day you will be able to share it with the world.

Trust in the process and enjoy every moment, because what you will experience over the next 10 years will make you truly believe that dreams really do come true!

Sending you love and light!

Steph

Xxx

SUZIE
MILLER

Suzie Miller is a playwright who graduated from the Playwrights Studio at the Australian National Institute of Dramatic Arts in 2000 and has a Masters in Theatre & Film. Suzie received the 2008 national Kit Denton Fellowship for writing, won the 2006 and 2009 Inscription Award, received the 2008 New York Fringe Festival Overall Excellence Award for Outstanding Playwriting and won the 2005 Theatrelab Award. Her works include *Cross Sections* and *Sold*.

Dear Me,

You just turned 13 in October and you started to write on Mum's old manual typewriter. On the first day of January you spent the day typing a diary entry describing what your dreams are and what you want to achieve in the year ahead. It will be a characteristic of the years to come that you keep a diary and write down what your aims are – and I promise you in doing this, those very things will come about.

You have a great courage and capacity to drive yourself forward. Don't feel knocked about when people criticise that and try to bring you down – it is that very strength and love of life that will create your path. While other people seem to have all the contacts and understand how the world works, the struggle to get there alone will make the successes much more interesting for you. And don't forget to help others when you reach your career and life targets.

I want you to know that you will have more than one exciting career; that you should keep writing down all of your feelings as you did on the first day of the year – your writing will keep you from falling into melancholy when it threatens. Most importantly I want you to know that despite not having access to everything everyone else seems to have, you will be the first person in your extended family to have a university degree, you will travel the world, meet and create the most beautiful friendships, and go on to be an adult who loves her husband and children ferociously.

What you should know as you forge ahead in relationships are:

1. That at 13 you have just met a wonderful friend called Helen. Hang on to her, stay loyal to her – even though you met in Year 7, she

will be in your life for the rest of it.

2. You will meet some of the most extraordinary people who will be loyal and loving, and who will be by your side through some challenging times. Do not let go of those who are authentic and kind.

3. You will also have friends and meet people who will let you down and make you cry. Let yourself cry at their loss but be open to what comes about after they are gone.

I tell you now – do not be afraid to love hard, do not feel anxious about speaking out wherever you see injustice, do not judge others harshly and indeed allow yourself to make some mistakes. Some of those mistakes will in retrospect be ones that are your greatest gains.

While your primary family can drive you nuts right now, know that in the future they are there for you and your love for them will grow and grow – they are very precious, they have shared your childhood years with you and watched you bloom. They will also love and care for your children, delight in their successes and be supportive during their challenges. Oh yes and by the way – just so as you know – those names you chose for your future son and daughter at 12 are the names they now have! Yes, really, your lovely children have taken those names and given them life.

You will find the relationships that are right for you – do not be in a hurry, do not panic about where they are – they will emerge when you are ready for them. Relish the women in your life – they will show you the path to motherhood and nod knowingly as you discover what it means. Embrace friends in your careers of law, theatre and writing as they will surround you with an intelligent and creative community. You will feel less alone.

Never lose empathy and always treat people with respect and

dignity, especially those who have the least power in society. Very importantly, also respect and be kind to yourself. The only things you will regret in the life I have lived for you is not taking action or holding back for fear of being embarrassed or for fear of standing out. Because you are still 13 you can change all of that, and indeed overcome that barrier. Be wary of shame – it will paralyse you and make you withdraw.

There will be some truths that you know deep in your soul already. You should listen to these and act on them when you know the time is right. Everyone might think you are crazy, and it might mean starting again, but you will find great satisfaction and joy in doing so.

Know you will live in many cities and countries; you will find some lifelong friends in those places who will change your life in surprising ways. Your life will be rich and filled with great joys and sadness. It is a big life ahead for you, do not be afraid.

The teenage years ahead will have you starting to feel 'different' to your family and everyone else – you have the soul of an artist and a sharp, clever mind. Do not hold it back because others can't cope with it. When you find those people who try to hold you back, be brave and go forward anyway. There will be times when you struggle with depression, when you again feel lonely in life. Know there are things you can do to take yourself back to your own energy and life. Talk to those people who you feel really comfortable with, take some time with nature and continue to reach out to the less fortunate in your community. Each of these things will make you feel more connected and will allow you to regain the sense of a warm and loving world.

Some things I wish I had discovered earlier in my life that I can give you the heads up on now:

1. Our parents are not always right. Yes, they made mistakes but all

parents do – let them off the hook and enjoy them, as they won't be with you forever;

2. Writing is not something only privileged people can do. Don't just do it in secret, show the world your passion;

3. Celebrate that love of Maths. Don't be ashamed of it, it is not as uncool as you think;

4. Don't stop learning French. It will be something you will want to have later in life. Oh, and pick up another language for me, will you?

One more thing. I know that typewriter of Mum's you are using jams keys whenever you type quickly. Do not worry: by the time you are writing for your living, there will be a thing called a personal computer that will have you typing as quickly as you think!!!

Love,

Suzie

TOM
BELL

Tom Bell works at the Reach Foundation and also within the media industry as a producer at Fox FM. He has worked on-air and off-air, always spreading the word about the positive impact the Reach Foundation had on him as a teenager.

Dear teenage Tom,

Doin' it tough right now, mate ... I tell you what, though, it only gets better and better from here, my man. Without giving away too much, if you look around at the group of people surrounding you now, just know that they're great but they aren't there in the future. You fall into a world that you already know exists but haven't found it yet ...

I know you always see the best in people. That's something that makes you different, something that makes you strong and unique. Hold on to it, even when you think people are shit, always go and look for the best in them.

You've got some epic shit about to happen. You know how you tell Cam every weekend that you're going to make out with Jas!?!? Well, it doesn't happen right away but by year 10 Jas is your girlfriend! Yeah, boy, you date the biggest babe in the year level! You have a really beautiful relationship for a few years and then it comes to an end, it hurts to end, but it's 100% for the best.

Year 10 is a big one, dude, you end up working for a youth-led organisation called Reach – I know it sounds lame as all hell but trust me, this joint changes you and helps you find that world that you always knew was out there. You'll travel Australia with your best mates running workshops in high schools all over the country. Then you also run workshops in some of the biggest corporate firms in the country, and you do it all in your own style.

After school you decide to follow a life-long mate Marky over to the States to work at summer camp in Minnesota – look up Minnesota, it's beautiful. Dude, this is the best thing ever. You party hard, like really hard, but you also fall in love with America and do crazy cool road trips. You'll end up working six months in Australia and six months in the States for a few years. You'll make friends at camp from all over the world and they will remain an integral part of your life.

At 24 you will buy an apartment with a babe named Lucy, she's amazing! You will fall crazy in love but it won't last. You will teach each other so much, and coming out of this relationship you'll step into being a man – the heartbreak teaches you some huge life lessons.

As this relationship falls apart you start a new adventure in life. Remember when you told your dad you wanted to be on the radio? And he told you that you never could because you mumble all the time ...? Well, you host a breakfast radio show in Western Australia and it is so epic, it's a job that you love to pieces. The only issue is that it's in WA. In the end, that factor alone drives you to leave and move back to Melbourne. You make the decision to be with friends and family in Melbourne as you struggle in WA with the racist, sexist and homophobic crew.

Okay, so get ready for this, though. You know the babe in the year above you right now, named Jennah? The hottie you and Andy talk about! Well, you don't talk to her once throughout all of high school. At 19 you date for like two years, though, then split up. Now, after seven years off, you two are back together, wildly in love and living together! She makes you feel like a hero every day. You worship each other and see such beauty in one another. Your family loves her and hers loves you. You have an amazing thing going on.

Oh, brother, there is so much I can tell you that you do. So much travel, making docos, being a best man, throwing great parties, creating greatness, but the best thing you do is see the best in people. Always continue to see the best in people!

Love you, mate,

Tom

TRISHA
SQUIRES

Trisha Squires is the current CEO of the Reach Foundation. Prior to joining Reach in September 2015, Trisha was CEO of St Kilda Youth Service (SKYS), an organisation offering specialised education, youth engagement, housing and social service programs to young people. In 2005, Trisha established the Broadbridge Fund Education Centre on Phi Phi Island, which assists young people affected by the 2004 tsunami.

When I reflect on myself at 13, I remember being concerned about what I was good at.

I loved sport but besides swimming I wasn't good enough to feel like I would have a career as an athlete. At school I enjoyed home economics (which I find funny now as I can't cook), PE, health and English. I had no idea what I was going to do at university or if I would even go to university. I was in the 'popular group' at school, but it was very volatile, as I remember there were weeks where I was the chosen one to be rejected and bullied. I would like to say that I realised that they were not real friends – but every time I was accepted again I would go straight back. I felt conflicted within the group as I knew there were things that people did that I didn't agree with or I would feel uncomfortable about but I still went along with it most of the time.

If I could give my 13-year-old self advice, I would say not to worry about the future and what career I would have. I would just concentrate on what I enjoyed doing and try new things even if I failed. Don't give up too easily. Don't let fear hold me back. In year 8 I remember signing up for the student representative council (which was considered social suicide) but I enjoyed the leadership and decision-making. I wish I had made more decisions like that. I would tell myself not to go back to friends who had betrayed me, and know that I am worthy of friendships – and that they will come. I would listen to how I feel inside instead of worrying what everyone else thought. Your intuition is almost always right, your gut feelings will help you make decisions throughout your whole life and you just have to trust it. Be OK with saying no to people. Don't be afraid to be yourself.

I would be more consistent – as inconsistency influences relationships but most importantly your self-worth and anxiety. This is something I have learnt in my adult life – as when I say I will do something to be somewhere, I follow through. If I know there is doubt that I will, I don't commit to it.

Now that I am a mother I would say, 'Always listen to your mum's advice.'

Don't take your health and wellbeing for granted, pay attention to your body as this will help you later in life.

ACKNOWLEDGEMENTS

Thanks so much to all who helped me put this book together and to all the contributors. Special thanks to my dad, Martin, and to my publisher, Affirm Press. And huge thanks to the Reach Foundation.